On Poetry

On Poetry
Reading, Writing & Working with Poems
Jackie Wills

smith|doorstop

the poetry business

Published by The Poetry Business
Campo House,
54 Campo Lane,
Sheffield S1 2EG
www.poetrybusiness.co.uk

Copyright © Jackie Wills 2022
The moral rights of the author have been asserted.

All rights reserved.
Without limiting the rights under copyright reserved above,
no part of this publication may be reproduced, stored in
or introduced into a retrieval system, or transmitted, in any form or by any means
(electronic, mechanical, photocopying, recording or otherwise),
without the prior written permission of both the copyright owner
and the above publisher of this book.

Designed & typeset by The Poetry Business.
British Library Cataloguing-in-Publication Data.
A catalogue record for this book is available
from the British Library.

Smith|Doorstop is a member of Inpress
www.inpressbooks.co.uk.
Distributed by IPS UK, 1 Deltic Avenue,
Rooksley, Milton Keynes MK13 8LD.

ISBN 978-1-914914-12-6
eBook ISBN 978-1-914914-13-3

The Poetry Business gratefully acknowledges the support
of Arts Council England.

Contents

9 Introduction

Part One: Reading Poems

15 One: Led by the Language
16   *The Flea* by John Donne
20   *Thoughts after Ruskin* by Elma Mitchell
22   *Lapwings* by Alison Brackenbury
25   Building a Personal Canon
28   Plath's Rhetoric

30 Two: Deciding to Write
31   *Being Fifty* by Selima Hill
34   How Black Women Writers Defined the 1980s
35   *The Fat Black Woman Goes Shopping* by Grace Nichols
38   *Brief Lives* by Olive Senior

43 Three: Heroines and Heroes
47   *More fun than Nigella* by Lorna Thorpe
49   Paying Homage
50   Grief and Elegy
53   *11 The Camp* by Moniza Alvi

54 Four: Environment, Setting, Conditions
54   *Digging* by Edward Thomas
58   Re-writing Colonial History in Rime Royale
59   *The Doll's House* by Patience Agbabi
63   Permission to Write on the Window
65   Naming Home
65   *Pepys and a nightingale* by Janet Sutherland

67	**Five: What Gives Me the Right?**
68	*Hiss* by Jay Bernard
69	Make Something New
71	*The Fitting* by Edna St Vincent Millay
73	Finding Your Place
73	*The Fall* by Pauline Stainer
75	Honouring an Ordinary Life
75	*The Bean Eaters* by Gwendolyn Brooks
77	Poetry of Critical Illness and Death
77	*How to Behave with the Ill* by Julia Darling
79	The Details of Language
80	*Gazebo* by Martina Evans
82	The Older Woman's Silence
82	*Lunch* by Lotte Kramer
85	**Six: Politics and Social Engagement**
87	The Poet as Witness
89	Social Engagement and Necessary Poems
89	*On the 70th Anniversary of the Warsaw Uprising* by Maria Jastrzębska
91	The Artists' Take
94	**Seven: Translation**
98	*A Bengali woman in Britain* by Safuran Ara
99	If it Wasn't for Translators
100	*At the Edge of a Field, a Pair of Shoes* by Wang Xiaoni

Part Two: Writing & Working with Poems

107	**Eight: Running a Workshop**
107	What Makes a Workshop?
108	Organising It Yourself
108	Working for Someone Else
110	Momentum

110	Keep Workshop Plans
111	Caution!
112	Evaluation

113 Nine: The Model

113	Critical Feedback Model
115	Change
115	Masterclass
116	Exercise Model

118 Ten: Planning

118	45 Minutes
119	Half-day
120	Full Day
121	Zoom Time
122	Two Days to a Week
124	A Course or Series
125	A Residency

128 Eleven: Developing Workshop Materials

128	Inventing Exercises
129	Set Your Own Boundaries
130	Collect Poems
131	Themes
132	Props and Postcards
133	Smells
134	Workshop Basics
135	Why Write by Hand and Not on an iPad or Phone?
135	Why I Use Models

138 Twelve: Working in Schools and Colleges

138	Primary Schools
140	Secondary Schools
141	Special Educational Needs

142	Case Study: West Sussex County Council Gifted and Talented Scheme
143	Case Study: Treloar College, Alton
145	What Schools Want

147 Thirteen: Writing Exercises and Prompts

147	Creative Dialogue
149	*A True And Faithful Inventory* ... by Thomas Sheridan
150	The Creative Power of Form
152	Is It You or Are You Making It Up?
153	Childhood
155	Here and Now in the Material World
156	Your People
158	*Zephyr* by Catherine Smith
160	The News

162 Fourteen: Identity, Words in Gardens and Questions

162	Identity – are you a shapeshifter, a boaster, and who do you eat with?
167	Words – the perspective of visual artists
170	Asking Questions – Pablo Neruda's final collection

173 Afterword

177	Endnotes
179	Quoted and Referenced Poems
184	Bibliography
189	Acknowledgements
191	Further Resources for Writers

Introduction

In the decade I was a mother with young children I bought a calendar with a quote from a poem for each of the 365 days to come. Sometimes reading a couple of lines was about all I could manage but it meant that in the middle of making breakfast, finding shoes under the sofa, combing hair and packing up lunches, I'd hear Emily Dickinson speaking to me from another century and she'd set off a line of thought that walked with me up the hill and down to their primary school. I was juggling writing with earning a living and bringing up children, was often exhausted, but even so, those lines attached to dates were reminders of how lucky I was, and still am, to have the means to read, write, publish. In the old-fashioned way, I stuck some into an exercise book and my homemade anthology lives on a shelf next to my desk holding its pinpricks of thought.

For more than 20 years I've sat with groups of people at different stages of their writing lives, experiencing the liberation of metaphor – a child realising they can find words for the other worlds in their head, a man or woman released from the constraints of caring, illness or addiction, from fear of the past and the future, from the demands of work, for an hour or so by listening to a poem and writing their own. Poetry allowed me to do this. And when I read for myself, sometimes flicking through an anthology, sometimes concentrating on a collection for a book group, I am in awe of human invention.

When I began to earn a living running writing workshops, this work kept me reading widely, looking for new poets or poems to use as examples. It focused me on form, on what worked in a poem and it helped me understand how we use the tools of metaphor and language. I used model poems in writing exercises because a mechanic learns to put an engine together by taking it apart. I remembered a big old engine from my Morris Traveller suspended out of its rightful place when the head gasket blew. A poem has to be oily and heavy too. When I embarked on this work, though, I realised how little I'd read. I've come to terms with never catching up, but pledged to stretch as a reader. It's humbling to face this truth about yourself, that however much you think you've read, it's not enough. The flipside is to enjoy the many different ways people express the world, and to accept that there's some writing you'll get on with and some you'll dislike.

The chapters in Part One are short essays that have come out of my reading. They explore how other writers feed what I write and that this is a continual process. I look at poets I read as a teenager and others I've come to later; I question the idea of a single canon through the lens of my own. I look at poets who keep me going because I admire what they're doing with language, metaphor or form, innovators and poets who answer back. I question what gives me the right to write; I explore how poetry engages us, enters the public arena and how poets extend themselves translating others. I hope these ideas will be springboards to further reading.

Part Two of *On Poetry* provides hands-on strategies for keeping yourself and others writing, from writing prompts to running writing workshops, with all the preparation they demand. I cover planning, timing and evaluation, different approaches you can take as a workshop facilitator, how to invent your own workshop exercises and what you need to consider in different settings. I touch on visual artists' use of text, where it meets poetry and how I've tapped into that fluid boundary. I include sample workshop plans, case studies and exercises. At the end is a book list and other resources.

I know people who write every day, others who have gaps lasting years, people who finish a book and say they'll never write again, many who are still looking for a publisher who believes in them. The poets James Berry and Vicki Feaver were tutors on the first Arvon course I attended. I'll never forget Feaver's advice, 'go deeper' and on the train back from Yorkshire, Berry's, 'have stamina, believe in yourself.' The many writers whose work I look at here are also testament to their wisdom.

Part One

Reading Poems

One
Led by the Language

It must have been around 1970. I was carrying three books: *The Mersey Sound* featuring Brian Patten, Roger McGough and Adrian Henri; *Penguin Modern Poets 8* featuring Edwin Brock, Geoffrey Hill and Stevie Smith; and an anthology of Georgian poetry, first published in 1962. I bumped into my English teacher. She took them out of my hands and then her comment shook me. It was vehement. Personal. I couldn't like all of them. The Liverpool poets were in direct opposition to Geoffrey Hill. I felt stupid and confused. I couldn't understand her way of thinking. I simply liked Smith and Hill, I liked Patten, Henri and McGough. I adored Dylan Thomas and Sylvia Plath. Hendrix was alive (he died a few months later) shaking things up.

The 1960s had chucked choices at 1970 that were too threatening. It was only 25 years since the end of World War Two, rationing ended months before I was born. Writers, musicians, artists were busting out of unbearable restrictions. She must have felt under siege, a woman who thought she knew what poetry was. I was floundering too, curious, drawn to the range poetry offered and that range was most evident in language. My teacher had been sold a very limited canon, poor woman. So I knew poetry would provide me with more than a rule book. Rumer Godden writes in her autobiography *A House with Four Rooms*, 'everyone is a house with four rooms, a physical, a mental, an emotional and a spiritual. Most of us tend to live in one room most of the time but unless we go into every room every day, even if only to keep it aired, we are not a complete person.'

In those few lines, Godden describes the range of poetry I wanted to read. I went through a mystical phase, reading St John of the Cross and Mum's collected Cecil Day Lewis. Around about that time Mum was doing English A level and read me poems aloud by John Donne. She particularly loved 'The Flea' – tickled by the metaphor, 'in this flea our two bloods mingled be ...'. Me too, possibly for different reasons, since I was being taught in a convent where my teachers' mission was to prevent sex before marriage. Here's Donne flagrantly placing those Anglo-Saxon 'sucks' in line three, words that read simultaneously as 'fucks'. How Donne fitted into the spirit of the sixties! Go on, sleep with me, the decade screamed and a cheer answered from nearly four hundred years back.

The Flea
by John Donne

Mark but this flea, and mark in this,
How little that which thou denieſt me is;
It ſucked me firſt, and now ſucks thee,
And in this flea our two bloods mingled be;
Thou know'ſt that this cannot be ſaid
A ſin, nor ſhame, nor loſſ of maidenhead,
   Yet this enjoys before it woo,
     And pampered ſwells with one blood made of two,
     And this, alas, is more than we would do.

Oh ſtay, three lives in one flea ſpare,
Where we almoſt, nay more than married are.

This flea is you and I, and this
Our marriage bed, and marriage temple is;
Though parents grudge, and you, w'are met,
And cloistered in these living walls of jet.
   Though use make you apt to kill me,
   Let not to that, self-murder added be,
   And sacrilege, three sins in killing three.

Cruel and sudden, hast thou since
Purpled thy nail, in blood of innocence?
Wherein could this flea guilty be,
Except in that drop which it sucked from thee?
Yet thou triumph'st, and say'st that thou
Find'st not thy self, nor me the weaker now;
   'Tis true; then learn how false, fears be:
   Just so much honor, when thou yield'st to me,
   Will waste, as this flea's death took life from thee.

(first published 1633)

    In this poem as a conversation, a plea, as irony, as life, I heard Donne challenge convention and, as Mum recited it, his mischievousness was transported to the sex and language debates of the '60s and '70s. In this poem he has wit, a brilliant metaphor, defiance and over-the-top drama, a situation I related to, because that's how I'd been brought up – men only want one thing and whatever it takes (even death or torture, according to the saints) you remain a virgin. The poem is argumentative, and like the patriarchal attitudes which were being challenged as I grew up, it's rather desperate. I hear the pomposity of middle-aged men determined to have their own way and below the humour I see the reality of life for young women, pressured into having sex. I was all too familiar with his desperation, frustration and sarcasm. Even when she's won – stood her ground, crushed the flea – he doesn't stop: that's what her virginity is worth, a flea's life, a smudge of blood. Other than the genius of the poem, what I also rate it for now is its ability to travel – Donne's acknowledgment of the girl's smirk. I can still hear Mum quoting it, her books on the table, a green bank of woods through the window. Sexual liberation and who it benefited was one of the battlegrounds of the decade I grew up in. The Catholics revered virginity so much they even spun a story about a virgin birth. My teacher (the one who scorned my book choices) discussing Angelo's deal in Shakespeare's *Measure for Measure* (if Isabella has sex with him, he'll release her brother Claudio from prison) asked us, 'What would you do?' 'Sleep with him of course,' we answered. Next day she told us she was afraid for our souls. Stylistically, the poem's rhyming couplets are still so familiar, so adaptable and energetic, as is its urgent address to 'thee', the lover. We recognise its rhythms, 'This flea is you and I, and this / Our marriage bed ...' as our own. It is pure performance, the poem has a mike in its hand and a wide stage.

Sister Short was one of the few nuns to teach us without Catholicism interrupting. I did my rote learning of Shakespeare to the rhythm of a treadle sewing machine in her needlework classes. So to a soundtrack of The Temptations' 'Just My Imagination (Running Away With Me)', Janis Joplin's 'Me and Bobby McGee', and Sly and the Family Stone's 'Family Affair', my head was filling up with Shakespeare's iambic pentameter, Chaucer, Wordsworth and the sung Latin Mass. At that Mass I absorbed the call and response, invocation, the magic of three, penitence, the mystery of the chant – Kyrie Eleison – the commandments, the sound of prayers recited communally, the alchemy that existed in music and words.

Then there was Sylvia Plath. I was eight when she died on 11th February 1963 but she was still a contemporary voice when six years on I began to be aware of her work. I lent out my teenage copy of her novel *The Bell Jar* too many times and it never returned and her poetry was essential reading for a literate white English girl in the 1960s and 1970s. I had no idea what I was missing as other American women poets documented the civil rights movement. The appeal of Plath's poetry was the psychological territory she waved as a flag. I read Plath in the same way I strained to understand Leonard Cohen's lyrics. Did my friends and I whisper the words to 'Daddy' in the corridors, thrilled by her courage? We saw the 10 couplets of 'Edge', the three hard 'ah's of that final line. She was more dangerous than tragic to us at that age. I'd come back to her time and again – I didn't know it then, but she became one of the poets who'd focus me when I was floundering with my own writing.

But it's salutary to reflect I had no idea as a teenager about the Black Arts movement and poets Sonia Sanchez, Nikki Giovanni, Audre Lorde, June Jordan and Gwendolyn Brooks. Plath became an icon because she was a woman. It would take me longer to read these Black women poets. And I know things are changing, but it still underlines for me how important it is to ask, what, and who, am I missing?

Reading Plath was markedly different to reading Rumer Godden's *The Greengage Summer*. It was one of the novels I most loved in my teens but I read her and then forgot about her. Although *The Greengage Summer* was sheer pleasure, it frightened me. Misery was expected of a Catholic, not happiness. Three decades later I began to buy every book of Godden's I came across in charity shops. I found novels printed on wartime paper. I realised why I associated *The Greengage Summer* with pleasure – her prose reads like poetry. Godden was a writer who paid attention, who was brave enough to concentrate on the domestic music of a house. I needed writers to speak to me in my own voice, we all do. Just as DNA is unique, so is what brings each of us to writing.

A poem I missed at the time I was first reading Plath deals head on with the canon and what it shows me now is the power of the myth of the Romantic creative, suffering for art without a dishcloth in sight. Plath aside, who did write about blackberrying and potatoes, nevertheless appealed because of her rebellion and initially, to me, her dangerous ideas. Elma Mitchell, in this poem, is addressing domestic politics at their grimiest and most visceral, setting 'him' against 'me' in the first two lines and women as 'they', an amorphous other, a group that's not what it seems.

Thoughts after Ruskin
by Elma Mitchell

Women reminded him of lilies and roses.
Me they remind rather of blood and soap,
Armed with a warm rag, assaulting noses,
Ears, neck, mouth and all the secret places:

Armed with a sharp knife, cutting up liver,
Holding hearts to bleed under a running tap,
Gutting and stuffing, pickling and preserving,
Scalding, blanching, broiling, pulverising,
– All the terrible chemistry of their kitchens.

Their distant husbands lean across mahogany
And delicately manipulate the market,
While safe at home, the tender and gentle
Are killing tiny mice, dead snap by the neck,
Asphyxiating flies, evicting spiders,
Scrubbing, scouring aloud, disturbing cupboards,
Committing things to dustbins, twisting, wringing,
Wrists red and knuckles white and fingers puckered,
Pulpy, tepid. Steering screaming cleaners
Around the snags of furniture, they straighten
And haul out sheets from under the incontinent
And heavy old, stoop to importunate young,
Tugging, folding, tucking, zipping, buttoning,
Spooning in food, encouraging excretion,
Mopping up vomit, stabbing cloth with needles,
Contorting wool around their knitting needles,
Creating snug and comfy on their needles.
Their huge hands! their everywhere eyes! their voices
Raised to convey across the hullabaloo,

Their massive thighs and breasts dispensing comfort,
Their bloody passages and hairy crannies,
Their wombs that pocket a man upside down!

And when all's over, off with overalls,
Quickly consulting clocks, they go upstairs,
Sit and sigh a little, brushing hair,
And somehow find, in mirrors, colours, odours,
Their essences of lilies and of roses.

>from *People Etcetera: New and Selected Poems* (Peterloo Poets, 1987)

Ruth Padel[1] has drawn attention to the fact that Mitchell had no women poets as role models when she began writing. This poem, first published in 1967, is a description of combat – a woman against a hostile regime of domestic demands. In lists of gerunds she underscores woman's relentless physical activity, the violent impact caring has on her body, her impact on the material world, the bodily fluids she has to deal with. The repetition of 'needles' three times is a curse and a promise that drives us to the womb. The poem details a mid-20th century English woman's daily duties and sets them against the same era's image and expectations of a middle class wife. Mitchell's women may be jugglers (they have to be chemists, surgeons, torturers, assassins) but ultimately they're reduced to gynaecology. This poem triumphs in its own language. The idea of the woman's role is a platform, but its conceit, beginning with such opposing perceptions of women, is to disrupt and disturb. The poem's extended third stanza gives the descriptions it contains an epic quality. In this stanza Mitchell focuses on the body, all that women do, their surroundings, a woman's inherent and permanent state of transgression. The form of the poem helps us understand how these grotesque warriors have come into being – from the first suggestion of 'blood and soap' to the short stanza exploring in more detail the 'terrible chemistry of their kitchens' we are led into hostile territory, shown giants with mythical qualities who never get tired, capable of overwhelming a man. In the final stanza Mitchell delivers an equally mythical metamorphosis, using the same pair of floral scents as in the combative first stanza, picking up the strategically placed nouns, soap and odours to close the circle.

Decades on from Mitchell, another poet who celebrates domestic life is Alison Brackenbury, whose careful eye in this poem explores loss and what we take for granted. I go to Brackenbury's poems for delicacy and quietness. These qualities give her language a different kind of vigour and tautness that come from attention to detail.

Lapwings
by Alison Brackenbury

They were everywhere. No. Just God or smoke
is that. They were the backdrop to the road,

my parents' home, the heavy winter fields
from which they flashed and kindled and uprode

the air in dozens. I ignored them all.
"What are they?" "Oh – peewits –" Then a hare flowed,

bounded the furrows. Marriage. Child. I roamed
round other farms. I only knew them gone

when, out of a sad winter, one returned.
I heard the high mocked cry "Pee – wit," so long

cut dead. I watched it buckle from vast air
to lure hawks from its chicks. That time had gone.

Gravely, the parents bobbed their strip of stubble.
How had I let this green and purple pass?

Fringed, plumed heads (full name, the crested plover)
fluttered. So crowned cranes stalk Kenyan grass.

Then their one child, their anxious care, came running,
squeaked along each furrow, dauntless, daft.

Did I once know the story of their lives,
do they migrate from Spain? or coasts' cold run?

And I forgot their massive arcs of wing.
When their raw cries swept over, my head spun

with all the brilliance of their black and white
as though you cracked the dark and found the sun.

from Then (Carcanet, 2013)

The rhymes and half rhymes in threes at the end of the second line of each couplet, and the couplets themselves, are typical of Brackenbury's understated writing. I like couplets for the space they produce on the page and the energy they generate, moving the reading of the poem on. A couplet, as we know from the ghazal, contains its own elements of a story or language, insights and thought. Brackenbury joins the thoughts and images with rhyme. These sounds are a thread and the music she makes plays steadily, goes deep. She doesn't make a big deal of her metaphors but uses them confidently. Between she observes, questions, revisits, explores the nature of uncertainty and memory. All this is so human and right that, long before the final, stunning line, she has engaged the heart, and with that image it is possible to breathe out again. How brave, she is, though, to introduce the word God in the first line, in the same breath as smoke and that word we use so casually, 'everywhere'. Hear how it chimes with air and then hare, this assonance emphasising a development in the idea, placing the poet's eye more precisely. In these words she moves from sky to ground and a single hare, far more significant because of its mythical status and its associations with fertility. These associations feed those single-word biographical notes, 'Marriage. Child.' so that nothing more is needed there. And so I begin to realise how much else is going on beyond the conventions of the line and single narrative. I'm fascinated by the ends of lines eight, 10 and 12, which read "gone/long/gone", the way other line endings like "run/spun/sun" contain their own condensed tune. I wonder if reading in this way is fanciful, but it also alerts me to the fact that the experienced poet composes on many levels, producing facets of meaning and sound from their skill with words, releasing them from conventional syntax.

On one level, Brackenbury's language is clipped, mimicking how you might summarise a life impatiently to get to the important bit, which is the sad winter. All the emotional weight of that season, that crucial time, is carried by the memory of the bird, no longer a massive flock, but a vulnerable and isolated creature, under attack, anxious, daft. The insight the poem explores in its final two stanzas goes so deeply into the memory that the 'everywhere' of the first line expands into a glorious image and the address in the final line with its suggestion of divine power, reminds us of that earlier childish question, 'What are they?'

Anyone who's seen Brackenbury read her work will know how careful she is, how attentive to the audience. What she gives her readers is sheer dedication to the craft and exquisite detail. What's also critical about her work, and this poem is proof, is its attention to the natural world. Brackenbury is marking the decline of this once-common bird: 'How had I let this green and purple pass?' and watching 'their one child, their anxious care ...'. The poem is mourning the lapwing flock she paid no attention to as a child, a bird awarded Red List conservation status. Brackenbury, born in 1953, is a poet I've come to read and admire much later in my writing life and it's the precision of her language that has drawn me to her work, as well as its deep connection to the natural world.

Brackenbury's first collection, *Dreams of Power*, came out in 1981, a time when UK poetry publishing was undergoing massive change. A year earlier, Linton Kwesi Johnson published *Inglan is a Bitch*, but the old guard was keeping firm control of the reins through prizes and positions. Brackenbury is an example of a poet who's kept her nerve for decades, continuing to publish while balancing work and family and who was one of the women who added promise to the 1980s, the decade I began to write. I can't change the fact that Brackenbury wasn't on my radar then but I can be thankful for her persistence and the poems she's writing now.

Building a Personal Canon

Time, change and chance have all played a role in the writers I now include in a personal canon. There are also individual poems – what place do they have? And what drives my collecting? Is it as random as the books I pick up in charity shops and is that just as valid as any other system? In May 2010, I read about a woman who at the age of 90 – an apparently "unknown" American poet – won the Ruth Lilly Award. Eleanor Ross Taylor's work was out of print. Clearly she wasn't unknown, she'd been in the world a very long time. Adrienne Rich wrote that Taylor's poems 'speak of the underground life of women … coping, hoarding, preserving, observing, keeping up appearances seeing through the myths and hypocrisies, nursing the sick, conspiring with sister-women, possessed of a will to survive and to see others survive.'[2] I'm reassured when I read women writing about women like this, affirming our right to explore our own existence. I used to think I had to overturn all of that, I dismissed it as a lifestyle I didn't want. But there are so many aspects to being a girl or woman that we have no choice over. True to this, Ross Taylor's poem, 'Woman as Artist', begins:

I'm mother.
I hunt alone.
There is no bone
Too dry for me, mother ...

> from *Captive Voices: New and Selected Poems 1960–2008*
> (Louisiana State Press, 2009)

When I began writing I was troubled by the notion of an objective and single canon, and it was still being pushed as a standard of quality. It manifested itself in lists of white men. It set me up for feeling I'd failed – not academic enough, not well read enough, not clever enough ... I didn't understand all the classical allusions, didn't know enough about form or grammar. The (so-called) giants of literature (often European) don't trip off my tongue. Thankfully, reading convinced me a canon is personal, not learned, and I hold it like a mix and match – poets whose work I know deeply, poets I've come across through recommendation. Some will be part of my life forever and some won't stay very long. Reading keeps me humble and looking, it keeps me questioning how I perceive the world and reminds me there are different perspectives. The critical and contemporary word is a lens – a reminder to be aware of ways of seeing.

Common sense tells me if I only read titles selected by judges or teachers I'm a fool. It tells me to be wary of trends. So I take recommendations from friends, I actively search and I trust my emotional response. Often I don't know why I love a poem. Some poems keep giving each time I read them, some need me to do research, and some need a few months, or years, before I rediscover them and read them differently, in another context. Some offer a transient sense of surprise, provoke a question, move me on somewhere else, provide consolation or relief that this writer's expressed what I'm going through. Even poems that are least successful build a framework for others that endure, where everything falls into place – language, subject, imagery, pace, form.

The work of Carol Ann Duffy arrived quickly on my bookshelf with its bizarre stories of modern life. It's difficult, so many years on, to remember the impact of her early poems. The first book I bought was *Selling Manhattan*. As I read it again, I realise her poems showed me a new landscape, a liberation from the self I believed I was under an obligation to expose. Duffy opened up the possibilities of being another person, of stepping into character. Her control of the stanza and the line gave us English drama, passion and politics. 'Warming her pearls' was the first lesbian love poem I'd knowingly read. The year *Selling Manhattan* came out was the year of Black Monday, the Wall Street Crash, and within the collection the poem 'Money Talks' still resonates in its chilling, unapologetic viciousness It pre-dates the film, *The Wolf of Wall Street* by more than two decades, but when I read it now, that's what I think of. Juggling registers, quoting the Bible, 'Money Talks' presents an assortment of depravity and human exploitation from gambling to arms dealing, cosmetic surgery and violence. What I loved in *Selling Manhattan* were the monologues, the speed at which she convinced me I was really listening to the next character who walked out of the wings of her book.

The 1980s in the UK was a Thatcher-tainted decade when cocaine and champagne became legitimate workplace perks for the few, while the rest of us were chased by mounted police. I realise Duffy presented my generation of poets with exciting options – she added to the work of women writers who'd opened up the world of the psyche, family dynamics, sexual politics, motherhood, the option of getting into other peoples' heads. Like Liz Lochhead, she gave me confidence to make things up. What snags readers and sometimes writers in poems that appear to come directly from personal experience (writing often dubbed "confessional", particularly if it's by women) is the concept of truth. Confessional can be shorthand for poems written as if they were lifted straight out of a diary. The poems obviously aren't – the point is they read that way and that's the device. Duffy's device is to lift her poems out of someone else's diary, metaphorically speaking.

Plath's Rhetoric

On the 50th anniversary of Sylvia Plath's death Faber re-released *The Bell Jar* with a cover of a woman powdering her face. It announced, 'We think there is a reader for this novel who will enjoy its brilliance without knowing anything about Plath's other work.' Was it so inconvenient to admit one of the 20th century's most famous women writers was a poet? Is the trajectory a writer embarks on when she engages in that 'other work' of poetry just too difficult to explain?

The apprenticeship is long, the reading necessary and intense. For many poets the writing practice is far less disciplined, perhaps, than that of a novelist with plans, daily word counts, expectations. The hard work a poet puts in is sometimes to keep herself away from writing until the subconscious mind has had its go and always to try and understand the mechanics of poems she admires by copying, not plagiarising obviously, but mirroring what that other writer has done.

In 1990, I spent a year studying how Plath's earliest poems were influenced by Dylan Thomas. I was doing a literature MA to focus my reading as I began to publish poems. Thomas and Plath's work were as much a part of my growing up as bottle-green school uniform and the number 19 bus. The space they shared in my adolescence gave me a gut feeling Plath had learned from him and as I read more about her I found it was true. I heard the sound of Thomas in her early poems and themes. I discovered how he fed her fascination with the fabric of language, pursuit of the image, but above all, perhaps the idea of the poetic; the deepest, most extreme motivation and behaviour.

It was exciting to discover Plath had borrowed some of Thomas's most characteristic rhetorical devices, ones he'd learned from the Bible and Welsh preachers: ellipsis, neologisms, apostrophe, anaphora and particularly hendiadys (chirrup and fruit: Thomas; ruck and quibble: Plath). George T Wright identified Thomas as the only poet to use hendiadys since Milton.[3] It's no longer so rare. In fact it's spread like knotweed thanks to him and Plath. Plath found her own style, which became as distinctive as Thomas'. And when the *Guardian* chose, on the anniversary of her death, to ask women writers what they thought of *The Bell Jar*, poet Lavinia Greenlaw wrote, 'We imitate her without having a clue about the technical genius that makes her work such a force.'[4]

Greenlaw's insight is the trajectory many poets take. We begin with a drive to write something that's never been said before, to protest, to offload, to challenge or catch the zeitgeist. We imagine we write like the poets we admire. Slowly we learn the craft, understanding eventually that a writer's indentured for life. I collect poems in ring binders and cardboard boxes, on my desktop, on my hard drive. In a pocket-sized, unlined notebook from schooldays I've copied out favourite poems and lines. I keep it out of sentiment, to remember the teenager who so admired Plath, but who, as Greenlaw would point out, hadn't a clue back then about her technical genius. The force of Plath hooked me as did the fact she was a woman in a world of poems by men. I came to Plath on my own and with friends. She was part of my growing up and we shared lines from her poems as we shared music. When I witnessed my own teenagers swapping music, ideas, images, books with friends, I realised I'd never stopped.

Two

Deciding to Write

Those poems of Mitchell and Brackenbury balance one another for me like a scale – so different in tone, in the way they speak to me. One of them tugs at me sadly, one of them shocks me. Both show me myself in relation to the world. Both spur me to action. As I read these very different writers, I know my writing needs the span they represent. I guess it's what that former schoolgirl, with an armful of poets who didn't get on, also knew instinctively. It's what I realised when I began writing – I needed to read and I needed help with it. I've read several poets who explore this drive and explain it in different ways. For some, building up reading is like being an autodidact – the self-taught person who gains confidence from knowledge. Others approach reading as a guide to craft. What's certain is that the writer who doesn't read won't last and indeed why should they? Reading is also an act of solidarity.

In 1985 I was working for INS News Agency in Reading. The office was above a chip shop at Cemetery Junction. My shifts were long, and if, on my way home at midnight a cruise missile convoy set off from Greenham Common, followed by protestors, I had to turn around and join them. I craved time without the devil of news and I also found that on my way home, at South Hill Park in Bracknell, the poet Matthew Sweeney was running a writing workshop. I signed up. It was my antidote to tabloid headlines. This was where I truly began to write because it was when I began to read. Not randomly, not by accident or for an essay, but because Matthew brought in poems he loved. I heard names I'd never encountered – Charles Simic, Theodore Roethke and Selima Hill, classic contemporary poems that appear in *Emergency Kit*, the anthology he edited with Jo Shapcott. Poetry became discovery again. Thanks to Matthew I read Hill, became excited by her distinctively British voice, the surrealism of her world view, her constant challenge to what I'd understood to be real and above all, her female perspective. Hill, in 1985, had just published her first collection, *Saying Hello at the Station* (Chatto & Windus, 1984). I'd avoided celebrating any landmark birthdays past 21, and 50 was my next. Hill made it sound exotic, interesting and not a death sentence.

Being Fifty
by Selima Hill

Being fifty makes me feel large,
large and cold
like someone else's fridge.
I harbour scarlet fish
and fat gold eggs
that men in suits
with hands like vets'
remove.
I never speak.
Sometimes I might hum.
Or very rarely
raise a strangled gurgle
as if I'm trying one last time to lurch forward,
to get my fluff-clogged ankles

free from the lino,
hone myself, develop a fluked tail,
acquire a taste for frogbit,
and push off –
paddle off across the world's wide oceans
like a flat-footed sofa
that's suddenly learnt how to swim,
piled high with jellies, cheeses, cushions,
fishes, poodles, babies, balding men,
swimming-pools, airing-cupboards, hospitals,
and tiny pills, like polystyrene granules,
people advise one, or not,
to start taking.

from *Violet* (Bloodaxe Books, 1997)

The poem has everything I admire about how Hill writes. It is literal and visual, deadpan, needs to be read straight-faced. It encapsulates the hammered-home rule of late 20th century British poetry – show, don't tell – so perfectly that she might be mocking it. From line three the strength of simile insists you shift from human consciousness to that of a fridge. You hear the 'hum' and 'strangled gurgle', believing them to be your own, you see the eggs, fish and lino. You break away for a moment to see fly-tipped fridges in laybys and beauty spots and then you let go completely, allowing Hill to pile whatever she likes into the poem because it's her reality until it dawns on you at the end that it's also about the total mayhem of menopause. You ask, why has no-one else been writing about those little pills she drops in at the end? The poem has a narrative I wasn't used to – while it explores the psyche it feels inclusive and open. She uses the first person like a good stand-up comic, to bring a reader into the world she creates, to induce recognition.

You have to read Selima Hill in a different way to many contemporary poets. She doesn't allow you to linger, she drives you through her poems, many of them extremely short, towards the end. Only then can you stand back and grasp a sense of the whole. Hill's approach is unique; her style recognisable, forged by breathtaking similes and the restraint of form. As well as this invitation to engage, I think her approach is closest to conceptual art. She has always lived among visual artists and the range of her imagery is startling, photographic in its detail, painterly in its textures, sculptural in its use of space. She is a poet of series and multiples. Her work uses opposites, division and polarities to build up a perspective on the human condition that moves from visions as skin-crawling as Hieronymus Bosch to uncompromising expressions of the feminine that foreshadow Tracey Emin.

We know Hill for the apparently bottomless well of metaphor she invents. Her poem 'Being Fifty' has become a go-to for me for many reasons, then. It places poetry in the contemporary material world of Hormone Replacement Therapy (HRT), of fridges, sofas, airing cupboards and jellies. It has a surreal desperation I recognise from absurd TV dramas, it recognises the 50-year-old woman and that woman's voicelessness. If there's anyone at the bottom of the social pile, regardless of ethnicity, it's an ordinary woman who's no longer of child-bearing age. Hill takes this woman's almost indescribable fluff-clogged ankles seriously, she doesn't name the pills. And because of all of this, it's tender. It leaves the reader hanging with that woman, at the end of the poem, on the question of whether or not to take the treatment. There are millions of lives behind this poem and infinite experiences, but I want a poem to make me think, to lodge in my mind, especially when it is persuading me that looking into someone else's fridge might explain society's silence.

On top of that, Hill's poems are talking points: they help me focus my fury. Soon after I first read Hill, I discovered other women writers I'd place in my own canon, among them Vicki Feaver, Jackie Kay, Liz Lochhead and Carol Ann Duffy. These very English, very Scottish, poets set a standard of honesty for me. Many of the voices I was drawn to as I read were close to the spoken word. I craved poems that felt as if they were happening around me, like Lochhead's 'Song of Solomon' with its celebration of the physical world I recognised, including, 'the whiff of / sour milk from her navel'. The poem's one of many in *Dreaming Frankenstein and Collected Poems 1967–1984* (Polygon, 1984) that I admire. In the poem, Lochhead explores our mundane and embarrassing anxiety about bodily smells that no-one wants to own up to, grounding a poem in such an apparently ordinary concern, confirming that there is no 'wrong' subject for poetry. Bodily smells, fleas ...

But the other attraction is that the poem's a contemporary response to a classic of world literature, 'Song of Songs', a collection of ancient erotic lyrics in the Old Testament. So Lochhead's 'Song of Solomon' belongs to a tradition that presses the reader to re-examine and reassess the literature we inherit. She urges me to consider what stories are not being told and the influence of stories that are. In 'Song of Songs', scents are used to praise, to embody the lover, to show the nourishment of sex. The woman's body is a garden of rare and essential plants. A reader of Lochhead's poem might not know any of this if they haven't read a translation of the original text but nevertheless the ironic tone of her poem is signal enough she's undermining the idea of perfume as aphrodisiac appropriated by marketeers. It excites me when a poet so clearly refers to another text, building in the potential for theirs to be expanded by the older text if the reader makes the effort to find the source. This is the writer rewarding the reader twice as well as being truthful about her source.

How Black Women Writers Defined the 1980s

The publishing industry of the 1980s fired me and women of my age. Even now I can recreate the excitement I felt by summoning up names of the time – Sheba, The Women's Press, Virago. On my bookshelves are lines of Virago's green covers and black and white spines belonging to The Women's Press. This revolutionary change was being driven by the work of Black women writers, particularly Maya Angelou, Toni Morrison and Alice Walker. Those years and the women peopling them compelled an expansion of choice, challenged the canon and led me to Grace Nichols, whose collection, *The Fat Black Woman's Poems* was published in the UK by Virago in 1984.

I loaned my original copy of Nichols' collection and never got it back, but from the moment I read them, her poems lodged themselves in my mind for the originality of their language, the new landscape she offered me, a way of thinking that celebrated the female. Nichols wrote about a woman going shopping, the horrors of Miss World, dieting and the meaning of beauty. I had never read poems like this – vernacular, charged with humour, deadly serious. They set a standard and stand alone in their brilliance.

The Fat Black Woman Goes Shopping
by Grace Nichols

Shopping in London winter
is a real drag for the fat black woman
going from store to store
in search of accommodating clothes
and de weather so cold

Look at the frozen thin mannequins
fixing her with grin
and de pretty face salesgals
exchanging slimming glances
thinking she don't notice

Lord is aggravating

Nothing soft and bright and billowing
to flow like breezy sunlight
when she walking

The fat black woman curses in Swahili/Yoruba
and nation language under her breathing
all this journeying and journeying

The fat black woman could only conclude
that when it come to fashion
the choice is lean

Nothing much beyond size 14

> from *The Fat Black Woman's Poems* (Virago, 1984)

I can't imagine the 1980s without this poem. It belongs at the heart of the decade's many political debates between women and men, women and women, Black and white, between classes, islands and nations, between the settled and the many diasporas. And where would British poetry be without *I Is a Long Memoried Woman* – a collection that signalled a new generation of Black writing? When Nichols gave the 1980s these urgent, perceptive and bittersweet poems she was in exceptional company. Her UK contemporaries included Jackie Kay and Amryl Johnson. It was the decade James Berry edited *News for Babylon*, an anthology of Black poets that included Nichols and her partner, John Agard. What sends me back to Nichols' Fat Black Woman poems is the expectation that a reader will carry the poems with her, take them out of the book and remember them in a changing room, on a High Street, or while watching TV.

This everywoman asks: 'Will the rains / cleanse the earth of shrapnel ...' and fantasises: 'Oh how I long to place my foot / on the head of anthropology ...'. She articulates exile in a world made strange by the slimming industry. The ease of these poems, and this one in particular, is deceptive. You read the poem on many levels: as anecdote, drama, challenge. You are invited to think about relationships between the earth and war, anthropology and violent oppression in a handful of lines. Nichols' efficiency is startling and in the phrase 'all this journeying and journeying' who can fail to remember slavery? The reader, like the woman, shudders.

In the languages listed 'under her breathing' Nichols takes us to the past and the future, predicting a changed London, acknowledging the woman's displacement but also her versatility and skill. Twinning breathing and journeying, Nichols takes the reader to the core of her poem, movement and freedom. 'Frozen thin mannequins' are the antithesis of the 'soft and bright and billowing' garment that the Fat Black Woman dreams of. Nichols' skill in planting the suggested monologue as a subtext to this poem allows the reader to accompany an increasingly jaded woman and participate in her disillusionment. From that familiar slog store to store, the word 'accommodating' works hard subliminally and the reader begins a journey without a place in the world. Things can only get worse. Two lines stand alone in this poem: the deep sigh of a woman who's not allowed to feel anger but is condemned to an emotion that sounds more like a rash and finally a line stating a brutal truth delivered not in her voice but in the emotionless language of retail merchandising.

In this collection Nichols gently, imaginatively, carefully, challenges contemporary Britain and its politics at a time when MPs in the ruling Conservative government were openly racist, some calling for forced repatriations. Nichols has gone on to continually articulate women's voices, exile, ancestors, the echoes that resonate from a place of birth, and renew her poetic treatment of them. What she showed me in the Fat Black Woman poems, and continues to show me as her work moves through geography, history, legend and increasingly environmental issues, is the holistic nature of writing. Nichols writes without limits, finding channels to draw readers into her constant questioning, her poems reminding me of the complex layers of the imagination she has herself drawn attention to, arguing against the confinement of labels. The gift that Nichols gave us was an entirely new view – she opened up our options.

Another writer from the Caribbean, Olive Senior, brought out her first collections of poetry and fiction in 1986 but it was a poem from a later collection, *Gardening in the Tropics*, that installed itself in my memory, perhaps because it was the year I had my second child and the first garden of my own. At the end of that garden, a flint wall divided us from the cemetery. When Senior gave the 2019 Margaret Laurence lecture in Canada, her adopted home, she explained the importance of the word ground – a place for growing food as well as burying people.[5] Throughout her lecture she uses the metaphor of digging and returns to the idea of ground truth – nature and history.

Senior explained:

> Real gardening can expose not just dirt but secrets and memories, as can poetry, it's a way to explore the significance of ground as repository of those who came before us.

Years after the collection appeared, Senior produced a glossary to *Gardening in the Tropics*, that includes descriptions of plants named in her poems, as well as explanations of expressions, words and history. I am sure Senior's belief in ground and what it represents are why the opening lines of this poem hooked themselves into my memory. The poem relates to so many different aspects of my life.

Brief Lives
by Olive Senior

Gardening in the Tropics, you never know
what you'll turn up. Quite often, bones.
In some places they say when volcanoes
erupt, they spew out dense and monumental
as stones the skulls of desaparecidos
– the disappeared ones. Mine is only
a kitchen garden so I unearth just

occasional skeletons. The latest
was of a young man from the country who
lost his way and crossed the invisible
boundary into rival political territory.
I buried him again so he can carry on
growing. Our cemeteries are thriving too.
The newest addition was the drug baron
wiped out in territorial competition
who had this stunning funeral
complete with twenty-one-gun salute
and attended by everyone, especially
the young girls famed for the vivacity
of their dress, their short skirts and
even briefer lives.

from *Gardening in the Tropics* (Insomniac Press, 2005)

In the municipal cemetery separated from the one behind my house by another long flint wall, there are many other stories told on the stones. Just up the hill, on my allotment, I keep a collection of flint tools that rise up through the earth – my allotment's close to one of the oldest causewayed camps in the country. During excavations of the site, four skeletons have been uncovered, including one of a mother and baby, as well as bones of at least five other people. A 5,000-year-old skeleton of a teenager was found during building works on a nearby golf course. When I was a journalist I was sent out on a story about a man who'd found a head in a Sainsbury's bag while he was rotovating his garden. Senior's poem holds so many truths. Of course the disappeared ones remind me of all the men, women, children who've been murdered as a result of the slave trade and dictatorships but the phrase encompasses anyone who's left our lives and returns unexpectedly, explosively. Senior plays subtly with the idea of the skeleton in the closet, the secret hidden in the past, but her image of the young man crossing into the wrong neighbourhood relates even now to gang killings and county lines. What neighbourhood in any city doesn't have a resident drug baron and victims? And so the opening lines that lodged themselves in my mind at such a charged time were asserting their timelessness, the poem's deep insight into all human suffering as well as the very specific image of the sheer number of deaths caused by invasion, slavery, colonisation that the earth holds.

Senior spoke in the same lecture of not finding herself in the English literature she studied at school, of writing without models, which reminds me of Ruth Padel's insight into Elma Mitchell's experience. Senior's observation speaks to the critical issue of the lens, the gaze, and comes back again to what drives anyone to write – is it to express what you can't find? Or does a woman begin to write when she finds herself in someone else's work?

In 1984 Sheba Feminist Publishers brought out *A Dangerous Knowing* featuring four poets: Jackie Kay, Grace Nichols, Barbara Burford and Gabriela Pearse. Audre Lorde writes on the back cover, '... these are poems I need to hear and see, as they are powerful and strong. They give me something I need, an affirmation of myself as a black woman, feminist, poet.' The debate about representation is not over – it has expanded, it has proved to be complex, urgent, essential as each generation adds layers to it. And it all proves the strength of being confident enough to build your own canon.

In 1987, the Women's Press showcased these poets again with some of the freshest voices in the UK, from Debjani Chatterjee to Meiling Jin, Merle Collins to Valerie Bloom, Amryl Johnson and many more, brought together in the anthology *Watchers and Seekers*, edited by Rhonda Cobham and Merle Collins. The anthology demanded that UK poetry reconsider itself. Meiling Jin writes in 'Yet another poem of struggle' (*Gifts from My Grandmother*, Sheba, 1985):

> the poems that tell of struggle
> are all written.
> And yet I find us writing more.

In her introduction, Jin explains when she discovered Maya Angelou, Toni Morrison, Audre Lorde, Kitty Tsui and Alice Walker, 'then I began to write.' And this is another powerful reason to read. Poet Kim Moore talks about a writer's relationship with reading: 'I think continuity and change happen very naturally in poetry when poets engage with and read other poetry. I think the ideal position is to maintain a balancing act between the two – which is maybe achieved by reading twice as much as you write. I like hearing the echo of another writer behind the words of a favourite poet.'[6]

To hear the echo Moore talks about you begin to understand how that poem works and you admire the poet's craft. As you re-read with that awareness, it's like standing in the street where an ancestor lived, unsure of why you are so affected other than you have shared an experience singly, separated by decades. The movement in UK poetry captured by Sheba, Virago and The Woman's Press is dynamic proof of the creative links between reading and writing – showing how a conscious decision to publish writers addressing racism and social injustice, exploring identity, exile and language, was a response to demands that literature echo society and bookshelves represent everyone, as Lorde explained.

It was the same energy that drove writing by lesbian women in the UK during that decade, illustrated by the range within a subsequent Virago anthology, *Naming the Waves*. These writers, in the vanguard, were creating a new aesthetic for readers into the future, at the same time as challenging a homogenised English literary culture. An industry dominated by white men believed they alone were worthy of editorships, professorships, prizes and awards and of defining who could be called a poet, the language of poetry, the subject matter of poems. Black women writers exposed the protectionism within the literary world and their persistence benefitted everyone. They kept going despite phenomenal obstacles, writing manifestos for change in every sector of society. In 2019 Bernadine Evaristo explored the importance of this time[7]:

... I am indebted to the female writers who went before me, whose pamphlets and books shaped me in my formative years and have travelled with me to my many homes over the decades; works that are stained with tobacco smoke, coffee and red wine from the days when I indulged in all three, and, while I have dispensed with thousands of books in my time, these and others from that era I treasure – they still reside on my bookshelves, grouped together to remind me that they were the making of me.

Three

Heroines and Heroes

Susan Sontag, just before she died in 2004, asked and answered the question, what should writers do? She wrote, 'Love words, agonise over sentences. And pay attention to the world.' Sontag is writing about how a novelist enlivens time and animates space. But when she diverts to poetry, insists, 'A great poet is one who refines and elaborates the great historical store of metaphors and adds to our stock of metaphors. Metaphors offer a profound form of understanding ...'[8].

She wasn't alone, obviously, in giving poets this role. Maybe it's forgotten sometimes, not just by poets, but by the creative world generally, when it flings the word poet around as if it's a hobby you dip in and out of. But the work poets do amplifying our historic store of metaphors, carried out so privately, eventually becomes public. The miracle of language rebooted is what I read for and one of the collections of poetry which delivered that for me was *Gorse Fires* by Michael Longley (Jonathan Cape, 1991). In 1991 I was a year off becoming a mother, I was writing and hungry to hear new work. In *Gorse Fires*, Longley introduced me to a new way of experiencing the sanctity of poetry, the power of naming allied with the importance of witness. How or why does one book touch you more than others? As with Nichols' *The Fat Black*

Woman's Poems, when I encountered this book I was immersed in questions about poetry. This collection became another measure, classic in its purity – minimalist, clear. It was a turning point. I didn't know it would end up that way when I first read it. Just as Senior's 'Gardening in the Tropics' often surfaces in my mind, Longley's title poem comes to me in odd places, especially the line, 'I am travelling from one April to another.' It grounds me, but initially, the poem from this collection that had most impact was 'The Ice-Cream Man'. The litany, the way Longley encapsulates the child's need to mourn, the adult's more experienced path of mourning, how in mourning we must also celebrate and how by naming we make sense of our world both before and after a death.

The other revelation for me as I've lived with this book is Longley's simplicity. When I was negotiating the geography of contemporary poetry as a reader and writer, four years before my first collection was published, it was affirming to witness this tight, clear language. Longley's work is musical and visual. He combines the qualities of these other art forms in his poems and maybe this is why he doesn't need to complicate his language. Longley's work moves me between earth and air, past and present and he binds it with love, compassion and understanding – lightyears away from the irony that often constricts English poetry. He celebrates life, sings about people with affection, devotion, gentleness. His work resonates with the *cante jondo* of Lorca or the mountain-sharp perception of a monk. Longley provides us with meditations, sets his images in the space they need to hum. His shorter poems define the collection and yet seem enormous. Among the narratives, they're spaces for humour, contemplation, elegy, as well as opportunities to honour the natural world, reminders to keep looking and listening while we can. The final poem, 'The Butchers', describes every massacre in a beautiful place and goes to the heart of the alchemy of *Gorse Fires*, which is that embedded in celebration are laments for people murdered and tortured. It takes courage to use lists and names as Longley does. It intrigued me for years. Then a few strands started to come together – Robert Graves's theories in *The White Goddess* of names as codes and spells, how a name is a thread through a family, the name that captures personality or is a gift of power, the archetype that a name can draw on. Then there is the way a list can be a prayer and a summoning up, reminder and surprise.

In my collection of vinyl is an album of Stevie Smith reading her work. I bought it as a teenager but had forgotten about her importance to me when I was growing up. It was her poem, 'Miss Snooks, Poetess', that came to mind after reading an interview with Vicki Feaver. Feaver reveals how her writing changed after overhearing students call her 'such a nice woman.' Miss Snooks was also 'awfully nice' and won prizes as a result. I never got rid of my vinyl of Smith. I carried it with me from home to Portsmouth, from Portsmouth to oh-so-many rented flats and eventually to Brighton. If I never entirely understood what Smith represented as I grew up, I am undoubtedly grateful she was present and that her warning was carried forward by Feaver.

Despite Feaver's profound influence on British poetry, she's rarely in the spotlight. It is possible she's the victim of her own success. She is quoted as saying, 'in a good poem, the poet disappears ...'[9] When I came across her poem 'Forgetfulness' at the Scottish Poetry Library I began to understand the meaning of a body of work. Like great women artists such as Paula Rego, Lubaina Himid, Etel Adnan, Louise Bourgeois, Yayoi Kusama, Agnès Varda, Noria Mabasa, Feaver has continued to express what matters to women. Sometimes quiet, generally surprising and always true, Feaver continues to enrich British poetry with her expansive imagination, like one of the women she writes about 'circling the world's oceans, and sitting / at the captain's table for ever'.

First published in *Second Wind* (Saltire Society, 2015), the wonderful character Feaver delivers to us in 'Forgetfulness' is a woman in mourning for what she is about to become, a Dickensian character in black ribbons, spools of unravelled film. It is a poem rooted in contemporary medical questions about dementia and how we describe it. But with Feaver's characteristic skill, we also enter the world of myth as a woman is cut loose from her memory. The poem is as evocative and uncompromising as Feaver has always been, demanding the reader identifies with a meeting of self with self. In a scattering of words she shows us our own fear, an archetype of old age we cannot fail to relate to.

Vicki Feaver was a tutor with James Berry on my first Arvon course and meeting her so early meant I made a place for her in the ranks of those who really mattered when I was starting out. She's always been present in my mind, urging, 'Go deeper', regardless of subject. Whatever Feaver writes about, she's wired into the consciousness of the greats (and proud to name her own heroes: Anne Sexton, Sylvia Plath, Emily Dickinson, Stevie Smith), into households of women, into stories we still haven't been told. In her work, Feaver strips language back to the most basic to release complex meaning. So apparently casual, her poems move from mother to sister, father to grandmother, childhood to old age, from toad to river god, peeling clementines to making crab apple jelly, and I accompany her because I trust her. She achieves this trust in a quiet use of space on the page – so that when a reader arrives at her most recent collection, *I Want! I Want!* we find she's mostly using stanzas of two, three and five lines with measured confidence, enabling the moths, horses, blackbirds, crows, rabbits and witches of her poems to invite me into her ever-changing landscape of blood relations.

The year I was reading Duffy's *Selling Manhattan* I bought Sharon Olds' *The Matter of This World*. Its pages are falling out as I go through it and find 'The Language of the Brag' in which Olds identifies the major difference between male and female poets – birth. She addresses the conventional heroes of American poetry, Walt Whitman and Alan Ginsberg, to make her point and sets down her 'proud American boast'. Olds has written ceaselessly about women's bodies, our sexual lives and experience as mothers, lovers, daughters, sisters – her trademark is almost forensic description of the body's fluids, shapes, sounds and colours in all its stages of life and death. 'The Language of the Brag' is like a manifesto, published so early in *Satan Says*. It tells the world the poetry a woman writes and narrates is as old as humanity. In this poem, the woman's body is monumental, a Venus figurine, and birth is ritualistic, ancient. Olds' job as a poet is to express the unsayable – 'swelling' repeated three times, blood, mucus, faeces, piss, the ritual ingredients.

At the end of the 1980s I saw Olds read at Brighton Festival. When she read a poem with the image of a contraceptive cap pinging across the floor, I had to honour her. During the interval, I stood at the bar with three friends, almost silent at what we'd heard. Olds published her first full collection at 37 years old. In 2012, when she won the TS Eliot prize with *Stag's Leap*, women were in a majority on the shortlist for the first time. Duffy chaired the judges that year and described Olds' collection of poems about separation and grief as 'the book of her career'. You have to admire the woman for naming her break-up collection after a Cabernet Sauvignon that can set you back £250 a bottle. I used to wonder what could follow Olds, whether she set a standard for writing about men and women that would be impossible for other women to match because her work is a challenge to writers, as well as to readers. That was then and a lot's been written since.

While Olds is a legend, Lorna Thorpe, a poet who began publishing much later gives the joy of sex a much-needed English vernacular boost in *Sweet Torture of Breathing* (Arc Publications, 2011). Thorpe is sharp, contemporary and not well-known enough. She's a writer of extremes – death and sex. In this poem, Thorpe enjoys sending up the British obsession with TV cooks.

More fun than Nigella
by Lorna Thorpe

in your kitchen the Sunday you burned
the eggs. You tasted of coffee, bacon,
my future. We were whipping up a storm
all that lip smacking and finger licking,
a searing heat as we jammed ourselves
against the fridge, tossing jeans, shirts, underwear

onto the wine rack. You basted
my breasts with coconut oil, I kneaded
and rolled you between sticky palms.
Breathless, panting, our desire
marinating all week, the wanting
so urgent I could have torn your flesh
from your bones with my teeth,
I could have swallowed you whole,
I couldn't get enough of you, our savage hunger
cocktailed with a soupçon of sorrow,
the angel's breath evaporating as we folded
into one another, your chin shredding mine
but I didn't care, I didn't care about anything
but that smouldering moment, the fire alarm
could have blared its warning
and it wouldn't have stopped me
from having to have you, from being had
up against the butcher's block,
the butler's sink, the stove.

from *Sweet Torture of Breathing* (Arc Publications, 2011)

Thorpe's poem stands out for its pace, directed by line endings, some hanging on verbs: burned, basted, kneaded, folded, others breaking the syntax so the reader has to keep going to make sense – the lines generally don't break for breath. Thorpe's witty title sets a tone so the poem benefits from what we know of Nigella's TV image, priming the erotic with the sexiest thing of all, humour. Set alongside Liz Lochhead's ironic take on sex, I wonder what these examples reveal about some of the fundamental differences between poetry from this island and the US. I wonder idly if a UK poet could write 'The Language of the Brag'? The only pause in Thorpe's address is 'a soupçon of sorrow' but by rendering cocktail a verb, she undercuts this too, as merely mixology, along with the angel's breath (for some a perfume, for others a brand of cannabis

– or is she referring to the distiller's angel's share?) She's chosen not to interrupt the 25 lines, presenting them in a relatively even rectangle of text, an open form popular with many poets. It suits a narrative poem, it can't be confused with the prose poem, it focuses on line breaks and because of that, it's a form that condenses energy. A vertical block of a poem signals it's not prose but it might meander. In this poem, so many lines balance on a new verb the action is frantic: burned, whipping up, jammed, tossing, basted, kneaded, rolled, panting, marinating, torn, swallowed, cocktailed, folded, care, blared ... up to the third line from the end with the poet's verb play in 'having to have you ... being had.'

Thorpe and Lochhead's poems belong to the category described as 'open forms' by Mark Strand and Eavan Boland in their guide to form, *The Making of a Poem*. They write about how the open form gives shelter to past and future and I like this idea of making a shack for your words and images. Well, not all poets will be content with a shack. Thorpe's and Lochhead's are perhaps more like tower blocks. In shaping poems we have to decide on where to leave space and when we can sacrifice it for the sake of rhythm and impact.

Paying Homage

Marilyn Hacker writes about Mimi Khalvati's *New and Selected Poems*, 'Khalvati's is a poetry, like Vuillard's or Bonnard's canvases or Persian miniatures, in which ostensible subject and ground are worthy of equal attention, where each word, accent, metaphor, resonance or full rhyme, play a necessary part and merit notice.'[10] In Khalvati's collection *The Meanest Flower* (Carcanet, 2007) she pays tribute to Hafez, a 14th century Iranian poet whose work is still celebrated. In 'Ghazal (after Hafez)' she shows how the form has proved to be as adaptable to contemporary thought as the sonnet, allowing the poet to return repeatedly to a word or thought, showing its many facets, demanding versatility and invention. In this poem, the most urgent word in contemporary terms – enough – drives Khalvati's poem effortlessly. It's a sped-up review of what matters, a poem of gratitude as well as a kind of manifesto moving between images of a garden, grapes, the moon, stream, market and big architecture.

Khalvati switches effortlessly between the general and particular, 'I don't want more wealth, I don't need more dross. / The grape has its bloom and it shines enough ...', an approach that seems easy in her experienced hands, but which is remarkably difficult. The intricate relationships she builds in the poem through this constant repositioning of the reader provokes me to consider the bigger picture, and apply it to my life. To start, she isolates traditional symbols of the garden, a rose, a vine. The poet doesn't need to provide all the detail – as a reader I have enough to understand that it's up to me to use this to launch myself into thought or an imagined world. So Khalvati draws on the ghazal's tradition of eliciting metaphysical questioning, which also lies at the heart of the poem's repeated word.

As I read on, I begin to realise this is a poem celebrating life's pleasures – wine, the moon, a shining stream and love. By the last stanza a reader who knows the rules of the ghazal understands that the poem is in the voice of Hafez. I didn't know this when I first read it and it didn't affect the pleasure the poem gave me, but when I did know I enjoyed the poem even more because I realised Khalvati was honouring and playing. As with my enjoyment of Liz Lochhead's poem, knowing more about Hafez deepens my reading of Khalvati's tribute, another reminder that reading is often a series of prompts to go elsewhere, as well as to understand why our heroines mean so much to us and what we learn from them.

Grief and Elegy

When Wallace Stevens asked, 'What should we be without the sexual myth, / The human reverie or poem of death?' he was, like poets before and since, asserting one of language's basic functions.[11] The poem of death comes from a place beyond words, territory every poet sooner or later visits. Elegy is at the heart of it. Penelope Shuttle offers a clue as to why – an elegy allows you to continue to talk to the dead. In her work, Shuttle has created an almost anatomical guide to the years that follow bereavement, the flashbacks, the moments that take you by surprise, all you can't talk about, crying in the supermarket. She began this exploration in *Redgrove's Wife* in which every poem explored another facet of her experience during the illness and death of her late husband Peter Redgrove.

But grief is long and adaptable, capable of mutating and overwhelming any of us. In *Sandgrain and Hourglass*, she returned to its creative power. She writes in 'You', 'I'm like the river drinking from her own cupped hands ...'. Shuttle's confidence and metaphorical stretch give us grief personified as male – torturer and companion – while sorrow, pleasure and happiness are female. There are surreal fantasies, an imaginary 'Royal Society for the Promotion of Loneliness' and a kiss grading machine; there are prayers, disorientation, the push and pull of healing. Towards the end of *Sandgrain and Hourglass* is a poem whose title speaks for itself: 'Happiness returns, after a long absence'. Shuttle describes her three collections, *Redgrove's Wife*, *Sandgrain and Hourglass* and *Unsent*, as a triptych of elegies for Redgrove, her father and a friend. It must make her one of the most expert English poets on the elegy and its versatility.

Also examining grief is Moniza Alvi's *At the Time of Partition*, a narrative told in 20 poems that read seamlessly, giving the reader the experience of a continuous epic. Here is grief on a personal and international scale. Alvi grounds the enormous movement of people between India and Pakistan as a result of partition, the violence and chaos, with family tragedy – the loss of an uncle. Alvi's always worked in the territory of the surreal and myth, and she draws on those elements too for her creative response to this event in 1947, the scale of which is almost impossible to contemplate – up to 20 million people displaced on the basis of religion, as a result of separating the British Empire in two. And as well as finding the way into history through family, Alvi has also spoken about the challenge of form in being able to write *At the Time of Partition*:

> It was difficult to get going until I found that it wasn't 'destined' to be a series of very short poems, but longer sections, loosely in couplets. Finding this fairly fluid form was a help. But sometimes because the form was so fluid, that in itself caused difficulty.

Alvi's body of work is distinguished by its minimalism – poems often so concentrated they appear to mirror the workings of an imagination that's always questioning how it can explain the world. From the iconic phrase 'Your body is your country' found in an early poem, 'The Sari', Alvi has constantly generated new metaphors to penetrate the realities of growing up in England with what she defined so early on as 'a country at my shoulder.' It's by no means her only material – Alvi's reach is broad and her collections touch on family life, relationships, work, metaphysics and everyday life through parable, creation myth and startling imagery. She returns to this desire to articulate the reverberations from a split world when she imagines her grandmother and five of her children as refugees and attempts to place within that enormity the moment her uncle Athar was lost. Alvi shows her family getting on a crowded bus with pots, pans, luggage, the political backdrop, the stories of terrible killings, until they arrive at the refugee camp, a section of the poem about half-way through that ends with the desperate daily search for Athar.

When *At the Time of Partition* was published in 2013 the UNHCR reported there were 51.2 million forcibly displaced people in the world – more than half from Afghanistan, Syria and Somalia. True to her innate ability to render politics personal, Alvi shows how close we are to this reality. Her brevity, creative skill and ear show us what we see in the news but make it new, contained tightly in these short lines, end-stopped couplets, impressionistic descriptions, and language like scribbled notes.

11 The Camp
by Moniza Alvi

A vast parody of a city.

Almost featureless.
Teeming, but not bustling.

Children climbed trees
to see where the camp ended.

Tents – and patchwork shelters
of sheet metal, rags and bamboo.

Her temporary home, precarious
yet somehow enduring.

Ludhiana, a lifetime away.
Lahore, just out of reach.

Ragged ocean.
Oh to sail to the other side!

Where would they end up? And when?
And with what?

from *At the Time of Partition* (Bloodaxe Books, 2013)

Four
Environment, Setting, Conditions

When I'm walking down the path to my allotment, I often anticipate the opening of 'Digging' by Edward Thomas. It lifts me to hear those lines in my head, as if I'm preparing myself to escape words. But of course, the poem isn't innocent. It brings far more to mind than the scent of currants. In naming scents, Thomas suggests the passage of life into death. He died in 1917, just before the end of WWI and his poem is heartbreaking in its focus on bonfire smoke, dark earth, the robin's song, when you think of the battlegrounds of northern France. He never saw it in print: it was published in *Last Poems* a year later, in 1918.

Digging
by Edward Thomas

Today I think
Only with scents – scents dead leaves yield,
And bracken, and wild carrots' seed,
And the square mustard field;

Odours that rise
When the spade wounds the root of tree,
Rose, currant, raspberry, or goutweed,
Rhubarb or celery;

The smoke's smell, too
Flowing from where a bonfire burns
The dead, the waste, the dangerous,
And all to sweetness turns.

It is enough
To smell, to crumble the dark earth
While the robin sings over again
Sad songs of Autumn mirth.

from *Last Poems* (Selwyn & Blount, 1918)

There was a time I was slightly ashamed of writing about plants and gardening, as if it was a lyrical backwater. But to a large extent, you go with what comes to you in the moment of writing, in the setting and environment you find yourself in. This is what feels honest to me. I don't know Thomas' work as many do, but I chose this poem years ago as a poem of the day emailed to people in a company where I was doing a residency. It was the opening two lines then that struck me, and it has now trod itself into the space by the allotment gate when I put the lock back on. It is a poem of place for me, as familiar now as the nettles that hang over and sting my arms, as the elder and then lime flowers that release their perfume for such a short time in summer. It's a poem that liberates me and reassures me that it's okay to immerse myself beyond language.

Another poem that I always think of when I'm weeding the herb patch is 'Zaatar' by Sarah Maguire from *Almost the Equinox: Selected Poems* (Chatto & Windus, 2015). It spotlights a different war – that between Israel and Palestine, and on dry, stony ground, the smell underfoot:

> Astringent, aromatic, antiseptic –
> the souls of the dead
> come to rest in the blooms
> of this bitter herb

Zaatar is a variety of thyme and it grows well on our downland chalk but profusely in Palestine. Even if we are accustomed to news footage from Gaza whenever there's another atrocity, Maguire's poem layers it with the smell of a kitchen's commonest herb and that herb changes in your hand. The volatile oil she goes on to describe, its pungency and her metaphor later in the poem equating pollen and gunpowder mean I won't think of thyme the same way again. It's always associated with Palestine. When I shop in Taj, Brighton's best Middle Eastern supermarket, and see zaatar on the shelf, I think of Maguire's poem. When a Lebanese friend with an allotment over the road comes for plums in the summer, she crushes it and says its name and I think of this poem. It is the most you can hope for, as a writer, for your poems to exist among strangers. Maguire, a gardener, understood the legacy inherent in seeds and grafting, the need for biodiversity. She transferred this, and more, to her poetry, to translation and to the anthology of poems about flowers, plants and trees that she edited, *Flora Poetica* (Chatto & Windus, 2001). I bought it for my mother the Christmas it was published and have borrowed it back from her often.

And so 'Zaatar' is an example of how a poem of ideas, politically urgent and engaged, lifts off the page. A lesser poet might have written something far more abstract, obscure and packed with cleverness. Every creative writing tutor underlines the power of conveying a story through the senses, and consequently, the body. We are flesh. Our bodies respond to the whiff of old cigarette smoke, an irritating rattle in the car engine, a fruit pip in the teeth.

I liked Maguire's first collection, *Spilt Milk* (Secker and Warburg, 1991), instantly. I read each new collection, and then I read her Stanza lecture from 2008, 'Singing About the Dark Times: Poetry and Conflict'. Maguire tells us in this lecture that in Islamic society, poetry is the highest art form and yet in the UK we have responded to poetry from Islamic countries with indifference. Her legacy then, is far more than her own poetry. Maguire's lecture begins with the British occupation of Iraq, the almost inconceivable cost of that occupation and from this she asks us to consider the role of poetry beside horror. The case she makes for writing poems, our fears in the UK that we are involved in 'some kind of arcane, elitist, exclusive entertainment for the overeducated' takes the reader (or at Stanza 2008, the lucky listener) to MacNeice and Brecht, to translation as the opposite of war, the CIA's funding of literary magazines. Furthermore, Maguire's speech explains clearly why poetry is so respected by Islamic societies and in so doing, challenges any fear that it is an elitist art form:

> This has come about for two reasons. One is the absolute reverence accorded to language because of the centrality of the Koran. Unlike the Bible which simply records the words of God, the Koran is God speaking to us in what is often described by native Arabic speakers as the most beautiful language ever written down. The other reason is that many of the peoples who became converted to Islam come from nomadic societies and for most of them, poetry is their only art form of significance. In a nomadic society, everything has to be portable. Nomads often make beautifully elaborate carpets, fabrics, jewellery and pottery, but the art and architecture of western societies has no relevance for them. Instead, the means by which they express themselves, record their histories and articulate their identities is through poetry.
>
> Our (peculiarly western) anxiety that 'poetry makes nothing happen' is greeted with hilarity, bafflement and incredulity by the poets I've been privileged to make friends with, many of whom come from the most conflict-scarred places on Earth such as Iraq, Afghanistan, Somaliland, Palestine and Sudan. They can't understand why anyone could possibly think that poetry could be irrelevant since, to

them, poetry is de facto, the most important – and relevant – art form of their cultures.

After a visit to Palestine, Maguire decided 'to devote my energy to translating the poetry of those cultures that currently we are so efficiently plundering and dismantling.' In 2004, Maguire set up The Poetry Translation Centre at the School of Oriental and African Studies where she'd been a Royal Literary Fund Writing Fellow. PTC began a process of translation based on workshops and co-translation, which led to the first publication in English of poets from many countries, including Somalia and Sudan. Given the communities of people within the UK originally from these countries, the British would do well to know their poetry, Maguire argues. Neatly, expertly, she ends her lecture on metaphor with Brecht's famous lines, 'In the dark times / Will there be singing? / There will be singing / Of the dark times'.[12] Sarah Maguire died in 2017 and we feel her absence.

Re-writing Colonial History in Rime Royale

At a *Poetry Review* launch several years ago when Moniza Alvi and Esther Morgan were guest editors, I heard Patience Agbabi read this poem.[13] It stayed in my head because of Agbabi's ingenuity in transforming an English institution, the country house. I remember it often. It expresses so many contemporary issues without being a tract. It comes from the heart of English culture's wealth, inheritance, popular culture, lies, deception, exploitation. Agbabi overlays the old deceptions with a child's fantasy world and begins to play. The girl's name, Angelica, is a candied sweet that only exists because of sugar. Ironically, the plant angelica is magnificent when it blooms and hums with bees, attracted to its honeyed scent. I've always believed the angelica on my allotment smells like paradise and now I have Agbabi's words with me in summer as I inhale. This poem is complex and layered, a lesson in history as well as craft.

The Doll's House
by Patience Agbabi

The source of the wealth that built Harewood is historical fact. There is nothing anyone can do to change the past, however appalling or regrettable that past might be. What we can do, however, what we must do, is engage with that legacy and in so doing stand a chance of having a positive effect on the future. – David Lascelles

Art is a lie that makes us realise truth. – Pablo Picasso

Welcome to my house, this stately home
where, below stairs, my father rules as chef:
confecting, out of sugar-flesh and -bone,
décor so fine, your tongue will treble clef
singing its name. Near-sighted and tone-deaf,
I smell-taste-touch; create each replica
in my mind's tongue. My name? Angelica.

This is my world, the world of haute cuisine:
high frosted ceilings, modelled on high art.
reflected in each carpet's rich design;
each bed, each armchair listed à la carte.
Come, fellow connoisseur of taste, let's start
below stairs, where you'll blacken your sweet tooth,
sucking a beauty whittled from harsh truth...

Mind your step! The stairway's worn and steep,
let your sixth senses merge in the half-light...
This muted corridor leads to the deep
recesses of the house. Here, to your right,
my father's realm of uncurbed appetite –
private! The whiff of strangers breaks his spell.
Now left, to the dead end. Stop! Can you smell

cinnamon, brown heat in the afternoon
of someone else's summer? This rust key
unlocks the passage to my tiny room,
stick-cabin, sound-proofed with a symphony
of cinnamon; shrine to olfactory
where I withdraw to paint in cordon bleu,
shape, recreate this house; in miniature.

All art is imitation: I'm a sculptor
of past-imperfect; hungry, I extract
molasses; de- and reconstruct high culture
from base material; blend art and fact
in every glazed and glistening artefact
housed in this doll's house. Stately home of sugar.
Of Demerara cubes secured with nougat.

Look at its hall bedecked with royal icing –
the ceiling's crossbones mirrored in the frieze,
the chimneypiece. The floor is sugar glazing
clear as a frozen lake. My centrepiece
statue of Eve, what a creative feast!
A crisp Pink Lady, sculpted with my teeth,
its toffee glaze filming the flesh beneath.

The music room's my favourite. I make music
by echoing design: the violet-rose
piped ceiling is the carpet's fine mosaic
of granulated violet and rose,
aimed to delight the eye, the tongue, the nose.
Even the tiny chairs are steeped in flavour
delicate as a demisemiquaver.

Taste, if you like, sweet as a mothertongue ...
See how this bedroom echoes my refrain:
the chairs, the secretaire, commode, chaise longue,
four-poster bed, all carved from sugarcane;
even the curtains that adorn its frame,
chiselled from the bark, each lavish fold
drizzled with tiny threads of spun 'white gold'.

The library was hardest. How to forge
each candied volume wafer-thin, each word
burnt sugar. In the midnight hours, I'd gorge
on bubbling syrup, mouth its language; learned
the temperature at which burnt sugar burned,
turned sweet to bitter; inked a tiny passage
that overflowed into a secret passage,

the Middle Passage; made definitive
that muted walkway paved with sugar plate
its sugar-paper walls hand-painted with
hieroglyphs invisible as sweat
but speaking volumes; leading to the sweet
peardrop of a stairwell down and down
to this same room of aromatic brown

in miniature. Here, connoisseur, I've set
the doll, rough hewn from sugarcane's sweet wood:
her choker, hardboiled sweets as black as jet;
her dress, molasses-rich; her features, hard.
This handcarved doll, with sugar in her blood—
Europe, the Caribbean, Africa;
baptised in sugar, named Angelica,

has built a tiny house in Demerara
sugar grains secured with sugarpaste,
each sculpted room a microscopic mirror
of its old self; and below stairs, she's placed
a blind doll with kaleidoscopic taste,
who boils, bakes, moulds, pipes, chisels, spins and blows
sugar, her art, the only tongue she knows.

from Poetry Review (2013)

Agbabi was commissioned to write the poem for the Ilkley festival. Harewood House stately home and Agbabi's poem were built from the sugar trade that itself was built on slavery. Move over Downton Abbey, and the nation's coach trips to the nearest house and gardens, where we speculate about life below stairs and marvel at tiny waisted underclothes, how short the four poster beds are. We gape at great kitchens, enormous copper pans, porcelain, crystal glasses, chandeliers, oil paintings and music rooms. Hosts of visual artists are now reworking colonial portraiture, painting and decorative arts as museums and galleries face up to the fact their collections are built on income from the trade in people.

I'm probably not alone in having spent a day or so wandering around an enormous building looming out of a country park, following directions from room to room on a grubby runner that keeps the public off the good wood, with each step witnessing the truth of the class system. Agbabi's poem enters the vacuum that keeps so many of us ignorant of the true financial reach of the British Empire and gives voice to a sugar artist making sculptures for Elizabethan banquets.

Agbabi builds her poem with rime royale (ABABBCC) mirroring the discipline of the art, its intricately spun structures, showing the artist's steady hand in the formality of iambic pentameter. She uses a verse form adopted by Shakespeare, Milton and William Morris over the centuries colonialism spread – a rhyme scheme favoured for the long narrative. But there's more at play here – the way her seven-line stanzas are grouped together to suggest six sonnets, intellectual and creative scaffolding that help us witness the truth of Harewood House.

The artist is tone deaf. Yet music and its language metaphorically run through her poem. Agbabi reminds the reader of the mother tongues outlawed against the backdrop of fine furniture and hand-painted walls. Then, as if we are listening to a guide, the poet's voice describes the final, miniature masterpiece.

Another innovator, Marilyn Hacker, has explained why she's committed to strict form:

> I've always thought that for me at least working with a fixed form – whether it's a received form or one that I've made up – brings the unconscious into the work in a more active way. You have to be doing something other than thinking in a straightforward linear way, outside the story I want to tell, the mood I want to establish or the thing I want to describe. There is something that is nonlinear that has nothing to do with either narrative or emotion that is acting on the poem, an almost mathematical (or musical) requirement of syllables, stresses or sounds that have to be varied or repeated, a rhyme, sometimes all of these things together—these requirements can knock one's mind out of the box.

Permission to Write on the Window

Like many poets, I've worked in museums and galleries using artwork as starting points for writing. In 2003 I ran workshops for vulnerable young people, older people and London Underground employees using paintings, prints and drawings in the Museum of London archives. This project became 'Faces and Places on the Underground', an exhibition of posters integrating workshop poems with images. It worked because the people involved were Londoners and images were chosen because they were familiar. We looked at dandies, pickpockets, prostitutes, prints of tower blocks and bombings, the canal at Bethnal Green, images of the frozen Thames and bell foundry in Whitechapel. Priceless prints were taken out of storage and participants themselves chose the 24 images. What stays in my mind is how well these writers were able to project their own experience of the capital city through historical images to accentuate that experience. The best ekphrasis enriches history and is a catalyst for ways of working that go beyond what anyone might expect.

The De La Warr Pavilion in Bexhill on Sea reopened in 2005 after a two-year restoration project. It is a Modernist masterpiece that just escaped becoming a pub. I ran a workshop there with secondary school students, making up colour names after work by British abstract painters James Hugonin and Ian Stephenson. I wanted students to look as closely at the sea and sky outside the Pavilion as they had done at these obsessively detailed paintings in the exhibition, 'And Our Eyes Scan Time'. We talked about conventions for naming used in commercial colour charts e.g. pillarbox red, sky blue, etc. Later, I asked students to write their invented colours on the windows of the De La Warr so they would be read against the view that inspired them. Astonished, the students began.

A writer may not need permission from someone else, but I saw it as part of my role, running workshops, to build writers' confidence to go anywhere and confront any idea, just as Agbabi has questioned an English institution in her time-travelling. What matters is the emotional connection a writer makes with a subject. Sometimes I don't know why I am drawn to an idea. Sometimes I only understand I'm deep within a theme after I've written a group of poems. And writers work differently. The Harewood commission delivered a place and a subject to a writer who'd already rehomed Chaucer in a Nigerian marketplace.[14]

I know of poets who start with ideas and others who start with phrases or single words. What matters is that the poem or collection they write is authentic. How does the reader know? The writing has to convince you, me and all the unknown people who'll come across it in a bookshop or online. And what does that mean, to convince? For me, it's when a poet shows what makes us human from the conversations we have, the surfaces we touch, the photos we have in our albums, the people we mourn, the slights we feel and the songs we dance to. And if we can place ourselves within this material world, we might begin to find words for it and our relationship with it.

Naming Home

Janet Sutherland's most recent collection, *Home Farm*, is a truly unusual celebration of her family's dairy farm – somehow out of time, almost an elegy for a way of life that's disappeared from Britain. Sutherland's work is not concerned with being modern, although it is, or with where it fits. Her work is concerned with communicating experience authentically – death, illness, pain, as well as everyday beauty.

Pepys and a nightingale
by Janet Sutherland

Pepys wrapped a rag around his little left toe,
it being new sore, and set out walking,
coming by chance upon his nightingale,
which called me back to mine. I saw the past.
To the rear of the farmhouse there were yews,
rifle green and murderous to cattle,
and once my father heard a nightingale
so out I went to wait on soft dead ground.
It's plain he said, plain brown, just listen and
under a hundredweight of feathered branches,
a nightingale sang, out of full darkness.
His heart, as all hearts are, disguised;
a secretive bird in an impenetrable thicket.

from *Home Farm* (Shearsman Books, 2019)

Sutherland knows the power of naming, and that a place doesn't have to be particularly beautiful or remote. Just being there, in the poem, is what matters. She makes this poem out of two levels of history, the ordinariness of the bird, and darkness. Her nightingale isn't Keats' Dryad, singing in 'beechen green'; she uses a quote from diarist Samuel Pepys as her invitation and reason to go into the past where nightingales now mostly live. This is typical of Sutherland, her imaginative territory often informed by fact or memoir. Pepys' sensory detail, so easy to relate to, literally sets us in motion. Sutherland's a careful poet and since she grew up on this farm, knows what she's writing about – the colour, shape and danger of yew trees. Then she brings her father's voice in, equal in the poem to Pepys. His own plain words are all the poem needs, an instruction to stand still and (for us, the readers) to imagine the sound. The poet hears the sound and sensibly doesn't try to describe it but widens the poem out at this point to allow us all into the bird's 'impenetrable thicket' with our own hearts suddenly equal to that of the nightingale, of Pepys, the poet and her father.

Sutherland's work is so grounded that she earns the right to enter this territory, as other contemporary poets of the natural world do also. How strange our lives have become when this 'plain bird' symbolises so much of what we've lost. Sutherland, like a handful of other people I know, is probably part of the last generation in the UK to have lived this experience, given how farming and the countryside has changed – another reason to read her poems. I was, however, heartened when a friend told me about a nightingale singing in a Sainsbury's car park.

Chapter Five
What gives me the right?

There are places in the world where the right to write can't be taken for granted. And when I think about my right to write, I sometimes wonder if it is a self-indulgent question. But it does no harm to examine your motives, your place in your community, even if you conclude that your responsibility is to yourself, to be truthful, to express what is happening to you and those around you as well as you can. For most writers, the past, present and future are unfenced. We choose where we go even if it is outside our direct experience.

In their remarkable collection, *Surge* (Chatto & Windus, 2019), Jay Bernard examines silence in the wake of the New Cross fire in 1981. This writer was just seven years old at the time. Thirteen young Black people died and 27 were injured while celebrating a birthday. Bernard uses archives to examine official apathy and vicious hostility towards the community asking questions about the fire and its aftermath. Two years before the collection was published, the Grenfell tower block fire happened. Bernard writes in their introduction, 'I am from here, I am specific to this place, I am haunted by this history but I also haunt it back.' In that idea of haunting something back, Bernard shows us how the poet can put themselves in a place that is meaningful by reconstructing it, and in so doing, make it possible for the reader to do the same, whatever their experience. The poem is an instruction on how to imagine this horror, a challenge to be conscious.

Hiss
by Jay Bernard

Going in when the firefighters left
was like standing on a black beach
with the sea suspended in the walls,
soot suds like a conglomerate of flies.

You kick the weeds and try to piece it back.
Fractured shell? A bone? Bloated antennae?
Flesh thigh spindle, gangrenous pet fish?
An eye or a tiny glaring stone? A seal's tongue?
Or the sour sinew yoking front and hind fin?
Vertebrae or fetters? Bedsheet or slave skin?

The black is coming in from the cold,
rolling up the beach walls, looking for light.

It will enter you if you stand there,
and spend the rest of its time inside you
asking whatitwas whatitwas whatitwas
in a vivid hiss heard only by your bones.

from *Surge* (Chatto & Windus, 2019)

This watery metaphor, summoning the sea out of firefighters' hoses – the title suggesting the remnants of heat as well as waves on a beach – is in complete opposition to the subject and for that reason allows the reader to enter this poem with no prior understanding. The poem opens with disorientation, the impossibility of making sense of an experience, the narrator reaching for answers through sound since all that the eyes offer is a 'black beach'. And then Bernard does what Michael Longley does in his poem, 'The Ice-Cream Man': they recite a litany, invocations to the sea and the dead as the commentator tries 'to piece it back.'

These details take the reader far from Deptford, to slavery and fetters, but in such a controlled way that the following image, a black wave, enables the next phase of the poem: enlightenment and change. Details of the poem are forensic and shocking, as they should be, the poem demanding an acknowledgment of the aftermath of genocide, racism and violence. The sinister repeated phrase of the penultimate line makes the poem circular but the reader is changed at the end, as anyone standing in that soot-blackened place would be, wondering why the walls remind them of the sea. In their language, both vernacular and rhetorical, the poet carefully manages what the reader hears.

Above the hiss, you think you hear shapes suggesting the sea, in tune with the opening: shell and bone. But you are now being further disorientated as you attempt to make sense, with a list that includes a 'thigh spindle' and 'seal's tongue' until you are completely baffled by language that sounds medical but isn't human: 'sour sinew yoking front and hind fin'. Ultimately the language the reader's left with can only be elemental: water, fire, earth – incantation delivered by the insanity of grief.

Make Something New

Grace Nichols, Liz Lochhead, Selima Hill, Sharon Olds, Moniza Alvi and many other poets whose work I love are innovators either in the subjects they write about, or the way they write, or both. I'm glad they've written the books I have on my shelves. Innovators don't necessarily set out to make change but to put something in a space – a voice that hasn't been heard.

"I'll manage," said Mrs Stiggins, and taking down the muslin curtains from her room, borrowed Nurse Bobberty's sewing machine and made Ameliaranne a perfectly lovely party dress.

from *Ameliaranne Goes Digging* by Lorna Wood (George Harrap, 1948)

Ameliaranne Goes Digging was a present from my aunt in Australia when I was five and became one of my favourite books, not least because the hero doesn't have a dress to wear for tea at the manor so her mother makes one. Erykah Badu uses the idea in one of her films – a cocktail dress made from a tablecloth.[15] If you don't have it, make it, has become a personal ideology. I bought a sewing machine for my 21st birthday. I learned to sew at school. When I was perimenopausal, bleeding into the sofa and not going out for days because the amount of blood I was losing couldn't be contained by any number of tampons and sanitary towels, I wondered where the menopause poems were. I wrote my own, fast as the rush of blood. I wrote them from the experience of friends and because the body is at the centre of so much writing I admire. I felt the urgency of what was happening to me and some of the women I knew. A connection between life and writing doesn't have to make writing autobiographical, but it does make writing integral to the everyday. Poems can slide into everyday life by illuminating experience.

One of my favourite poems by Edna St Vincent Millay is 'The Fitting' because the experience is so female (but not exclusively). Millay's work is drenched in longing, always summoning up another place, another person, a need to dig deeper and deeper, to mine every moment in case it's snatched away. All of this is in 'The Fitting' but it's an ordinary situation – a woman is having a dress altered because she's lost weight – and from that the whole poem is charged with the unspoken story of a love affair. It's a brilliantly sexy poem and quietly done. Millay was as much a craftswoman as the seamstress described here. The music starts early in the assonance of 'maigri' and 'teeth', the full rhymes of 'hip', 'lip' and 'rip'. It's present in the untranslated French, in the smell of sweat and the seamstress' knuckles against the narrator's breast. It's present in the speaker's secret.

The Fitting
by Edna St Vincent Millay

The fitter said, *"Madame, vous avez maigri,"*
And pinched together a handful of skirt at my hip.
"Tant mieux," I said, and looked away slowly, and took my
    under-lip
Softly between my teeth.
                      Rip—rip!
Out came the seam, and was pinned together in another
    place.
She knelt before me, a hardworking woman with a familiar
    and unknown face.
Dressed in linty black, very tight in the arm's-eye and smell-
    ing of sweat.
She rose, lifting my arm, and set her cold shears against
    me,—snip-snip;
Her knuckles gouged my breast. My drooped eye lifted
    to my guarded eyes in the glass, and glanced away as
    from someone they had never met.

"Ah, que madame a maigri!" cried the vendeuse, coming in
    with dresses over her arm.
"C'est la chaleur," I said, looking out into the sunny tops of
    the horse-chestnuts—and indeed it was very warm.

I stood for a long time so, looking out into the afternoon,
    thinking of the evening and you ...

> While they murmured busily in the distance, turning me,
> touching my secret body, doing what they were paid
> to do.

(from *Poetry Magazine*, October 1938)

I'm sure that, even though most women in the northern hemisphere don't make or alter clothes now, the intimacy of this poem is still as potent. I've never been to a dressmaker, but I know enough about sewing to feel the impact of this work on a reader. From the start of the poem, the reader is aware of the speaker's body as the fitter pinches the woman's hip. We feel the flesh of the lip pinched too, the cold of the scissors, breasts pushed out of place – all of this detail insisting the reader is there, in the fitting room, feeling the heat. And having captured you, physically, Millay takes you to horse-chestnuts and an unidentified lover who's caused the speaker to lose weight. But more present in the poem and more real, are the women accomplices and witnesses. The poem shows us what women know about each other, how women close ranks, what doesn't need to be said. I've often wondered about the impact of that final phrase 'doing what they were paid / to do.' Class is acknowledged quietly – Millay doesn't shrink from confronting the differences between the women, but in the poem only women truly know the speaker's body, truly claim it.

Millay uses speech to distinguish the external and internal worlds of the poem. The French changes the rhythm of the language and the lines, literally adds drama, as if in a script. I enjoy the fact there's no translation and the rise and fall of the poem – the first and third stanzas with this different music in, the second and fourth, inward looking and reflective. In the final stanza, the narrator addresses her lover, almost in passing, but this slighting address is enough for me, reading, to be in no doubt that this is an affair still in its dangerous, obsessive beginnings.

Finding Your Place

Counting the number of Pauline Stainer's collections I have on my bookshelf, I realise when I think of her it is because I'm in need of a different kind of wonder.

> I am wary of explaining poetry. Metaphor is a dark and arterial currency. We sleep-walk into the well. What absorbs me is incarnating the image; finding the context where the scarlet particle jumps that free fall between writer and reader, and the sparking chamber ignites.
>
> from *Don't Ask Me What I Mean*,
> eds Clare Brown and Don Paterson (Picador, 2003)

Stainer is writing about her first collection, *The Honeycomb* (Bloodaxe Books, 1997). She lived for a long time in the Orkney islands, but even before that she was giving us images of skaters, bleached bone, fishing, ice and stillness. Compared to a more narrative poet, when the poem fills the page and you're satisfied, reading Stainer you have to be prepared to leave the poem and look something up. In this poem it helps to know spindrift is spray from the crests of waves during a gale, haar is a sea fog, shrouds are also fog.

The Fall
by Pauline Stainer

That autumn
there was a fall of goldcrests
on the island.

They came through spindrift
like winnowed grain
wave after wave

exhausted, silent
thicker than leaves
on the rigging in North Bay

not even the burn of them
off the water
between midnight and morning.

And when the haar rose
from the shrouds
they were gone

migrating very fast
over slow shipwrecks
into the sun.

from *Parable Island* (Bloodaxe Books, 1999)

The reason I go back to this poem or remember it at odd moments is the intensity and magnificence of the image of these tiny migrating birds, and Stainer's use of the collective noun, fall, so perfect given their exhaustion. So much happens in this short poem and there are several assumptions that the reader knows what's meant. The choice of words is efficient – spindrift tells us they're sheltering from a gale. This is the smallest bird, as small as a wren, and it's migrating thousands of miles from and to forests. Stainer conveys astonishment, rightly, at this event, turning rigging into trees. I stood on the Downs near home once when three waves of house-martins went overhead, migrating south. The sight of so many birds, 'wave after wave', is unforgettable. Stainer shows us transformation not just once, but twice as a result and leaves us, as readers, uplifted, sure of the birds' future as they leave shrouds and shipwrecks behind. The metaphor of migration is placed in front of the reader without comment as integral to the poem. It works with those key words, winnowed, fall, burn, shroud and shipwreck. The birds' disorientation reminds us of ourselves. The beauty and intensity, colour and devotion in Stainer's poems make me think of the mosaics in the Basilica San Vitale in Ravenna, full of plants, gold and birds.

Honouring an Ordinary Life

The voice I listen for is sometimes just a response to something inside I haven't articulated yet. Each poet has her own way of talking back to this voice and for some it's in a dedication to form, to a sequence, to constraints that distract the too-hard trying mind. Some poets return to the same territory over a lifetime, turning it over for new metaphors or different ways to use the old ones. Sometimes I've heard this voice when I'm bored, when I don't have a notebook on me, when I'm too furious to sit still. And when a poem suggests itself but I ignore it, then I tell myself that if it's worthwhile it'll come back. Nowadays, I am just as interested in the voice that encourages me to read and discover poets who for years have been hidden from me. I have a residency and a workshop on writing about food, plus a lifetime of vegetarianism to thank for an introduction to Gwendolyn Brooks' famous poem, 'The Bean Eaters'. It seems Brooks herself wasn't entirely happy that she was so well known for this poem, especially in the light of her intensely political work. But as a reader I see this poem as political in the way that it stops me and makes me consider. Perhaps over the decades the poem has accumulated more power.

The Bean Eaters
by Gwendolyn Brooks

They eat beans mostly, this old yellow pair.
Dinner is a casual affair.
Plain chipware on a plain and creaking wood,
Tin flatware.

Two who are Mostly Good.
Two who have lived their day,
But keep on putting on their clothes
And putting things away.

And remembering ...
Remembering, with twinklings and twinges,
As they lean over the beans in their rented back room that
       is full of beads and receipts and dolls and cloths,
          tobacco crumbs, vases and fringes.

from *Selected Poems* (Harper & Row, 1963)

    I didn't grow up knowing Brooks' work. No-one I knew stopped me and said, Have you read Gwendolyn Brooks? No-one insisted I couldn't write without reading her. I've read her poems to reading groups and people have asked, why don't we know about her? This poem first appeared in the American magazine, *Poetry*, in 1959, alongside Sylvia Plath. She began publishing as a teenager and was the first Black writer to win the Pulitzer Prize. She was an activist and wrote passionately about Black consciousness. So is this why I didn't know about Brooks?

    There are many of her poems I re-read – political, devastating insights into race and class. But I am sentimental, too, and I've grown to love 'this old yellow pair' who Brooks describes with such tenderness, and yet partially dismisses later. Their 'chipware', 'flatwear', their 'rented back room' and its list of possessions, allow me to look at them through a window and believe I might know them, and perhaps exchange a muted 'hello'. In the tenderness, though, Brooks doesn't hide their poverty, the stamina and morality that have kept them alive and the acceptance of their situation, 'Two who are Mostly Good ...'. What's more, Brooks introduces racial consciousness into the poem immediately with the term 'yellow', so that this apparently simple scene is imbued, in one word, with centuries of meaning and history. And by suggesting I might be able to look in through their window, I wonder if Brooks is also questioning why their life would be so much on show. What is it about poverty that precludes privacy? Critics have pointed out how Brooks' poems challenge what is seen as beautiful and here, in this still-life, we have as calm and perfect a rendering of the mundane as is possible. The collection this poem gave its name to was pivotal in Brooks' oeuvre, containing poems about the murder of Emmett Till, white men in Westerns, and wealthy women dispensing charity. This poem rests among violence and moral chaos with its own integrity.

Brooks' genius manifests itself in many ways, but what I learn from her work is the importance of emotional connection and truth. She can be devastating as well as tender but she loved people. It is tempting, because of her long career, to think of Brooks as belonging to a different time, but as Poet Laureate of Illinois she apparently encouraged the poetry of a young Kanye West – her social commitment existed in developing others as well as in her own work.

Poetry of Critical Illness and Death

While she was dying, in her blog, in two collections of poems and in an anthology she edited, Julia Darling explored terminal illness, the language we use, and how to live. Darling's blog has been maintained as a celebration of her life and work. Her determination to write through the process has enabled beautiful poems exploring the time between diagnosis and death that for many of us is a minefield of taboos.

How to Behave With The Ill
by Julia Darling

Approach us assertively, try not to
cringe or sidle, it makes us fearful.

Rather walk straight up and smile.
Do not touch us unless invited,
particularly don't squeeze upper arms,
or try to hold our hands. Keep your head erect.
Don't bend down, or lower your voice.
Speak evenly. Don't say
'How are you?' in an underlined voice.
Don't say, I heard that you were very ill.
This makes the poorly paranoid.
Be direct, say 'How's your cancer?'
Try not to say how well we look
compared to when you met in Safeway's.
Please don't cry, or get emotional,
and say how dreadful it all is.
Also (and this is hard I know)
try not to ignore the ill, or to scurry
past, muttering about a bus, the bank.
Remember that this day might be your last
and that it is a miracle that any of us
stands up, breathes, behaves at all.

from *Indelible, Miraculous: The collected poems of Julia Darling*
(Arc Publications, 2015)

When I read this poem, I put myself in the living room of a great friend joking about the delights of morphine. One of Darling's many skills is the lightness of her language and the gentle irony beneath these lines. If there's a category for instructional poems, this must be an example of the best: 'don't squeeze upper arms ...' and 'this day might be your last ...'. She takes us, in the poem, to places where we might bump into someone who is dying, the everyday social situations that have changed forever for that friend or acquaintance. But the poem widens. The experience it describes to start with has opposing sides – it sets one way of behaving against another, it shows us the person who is well and the person who isn't, the awkward dynamic between them. And in the last three lines, we are all included – this is a poem that unifies people to celebrate life.

Darling knew from a lifetime of writing that metaphor is a way to understand complexity – emotional and practical. A poem can offer a non-medical insight into someone's suffering that a poet might spend years attempting to express. So if a medical professional has a grasp of metaphor, imagine how that could transform a discussion with a patient, indeed anyone who needs to take in complex information at a time of stress when he or she can't concentrate. Metaphor translates for us and Darling's poem underscores one of the most difficult things to understand when you are healthy and happy, agile and mobile – how do you understand illness and agony? If the poet's role is to generate metaphors for modern life, it is also to enable empathy, to explore the emotional territory that so often is only expressed in clichés.

I first met Julia Darling when we were both reading at a poetry festival of the kind that brought poets and audience together seamlessly – no green room or star treatment, most of us went to each others' readings and saw it as a chance to get to know some new work. However big or small a festival can be like a great bookshop – the perfect place to browse. It reminds me of walking by the River Shannon with Marilyn Hacker's Seine poems on my mind, along with Langston Hughes' line, 'I've known rivers ...', when I was in Limerick for the annual poetry festival, Cuisle, and enjoying an October river offering me its swans, wagtails, gulls. I could have walked all morning and wondered about the discussions between water and mud, a bridge and cormorant. All fanciful, but that's where festivals take you, to ideas sparked by listening, to being reminded you are part of a community.

The Details of Language

Darling's poem examines the choice of words in everyday conversation and this is what appeals to me in the work of the poet Martina Evans, who has some of the best collection titles in the business – *Can Dentists Be Trusted?* and *All Alcoholics are Charmers* (Carcanet, 2004 and 1998 respectively). In her work she's perfected a deceptively anecdotal tone so that when you listen to her you believe you're in a conversation, that she's letting you into a secret and that this poem you're hearing is for you alone. On the page the poem peels away to fill itself with sound. One of the reasons for this, I think, is that she is fascinated with how people talk, with the words and phrases we pick up from childhood that become part of our personalities. She's like a linguistic archaeologist. But this close attention to people also makes her poems, however funny some of them are, compassionate. She looks closely, she listens and she has a gift for recreating the certainties of a child's imaginative life.

Gazebo
by Martina Evans

Gazebo was the word my mother
used to describe a mad exhibitionist
or a queer hawk. For example,
so-and-so was going around
like a right gazebo. Naturally I imagined
a gazebo had legs and travelled, so
I was surprised to see my first one
on an English village green, going
nowhere, the wedding couple
toasting each other under its rippling
blue and white canopy as cricket bats
smacked slowly in the heat.
My mother grew up near landed gentry
and the gazebos hidden in their walled gardens
must have entered her language
like escaped seeds,

growing into wild tramps,
that straggled along the Rathkeale Road,
on strange, overblown feet.

from *Burnfort, Las Vegas* (Anvil Press Poetry, 2014)

When the poem begins I remember my father shouting 'pinhead' at drivers who annoyed him, me in the back of an old black Ford wondering what it meant and where it came from. Evans opens the storehouse of childhood and turns the poem into a moment of understanding that enables her to take us further into her mother's world, speculatively, and then the shared memory of tramps, far more exotic and theatrical than any mad exhibitionist. The final image is dreamlike and embedded in the drive of the poem to share the strangeness of the word, gazebo – the mother delighting in its sound, the daughter taking its meaning on trust. Gently, the poem underlines differences in class, challenges the image of an English idyll so the untidy and freedom-loving tramps have the last word, as they should, being nomads. Evans' poetry is both documentary and intimate, covering the Ireland of her childhood and forefathers.

The poem underlines our responsibility as poets to the detail of language. Here, the single word is all the poet needs to create a shared experience, as well as to go to the heart of what poetry is. There are many poetry theorists but I like Emily Dickinson's idea of poetry taking the top of my head off and of poetry transporting me.[16] Chase Twitchell's idea, too, which is condensed into the end of her poem 'Architecture': 'Poetry's not window cleaning. / It breaks the glass.' (*The Snow Watcher*, Bloodaxe Books, 1999).

Evans's poem takes me to the heart of what we do – she shows me the energy in our relationship with words, their function in memory and emotion, how a single word, like an object, can contain elements of a life and a personal history. Evans teases out of that strange sounding word, gazebo, the possible humour in its etymology, the colonialism suggested by its role in the gardens of the wealthy, taking us further away as the poem progresses to the lives of nomadic people, suggesting an entirely different view of life, freer and more involved with the natural world. All of this is layered below the first role of the word gazebo in the poem, to show us the infinitely creative function of language as language interrogates itself, as a word sparks connections in our minds, as a child rolls a word around in her mouth and in the absence of meaning, builds one of her own.

The Older Woman's Silence

And the next poem by Lotte Kramer also illustrates what words can express even when they are almost whittled away. Kramer wrote many poems about women's lives and about living with two languages, but she is best known for her writing as a survivor of the Holocaust, exiled in the UK as a teenager. Kramer worked in a laundry, as a lady's companion, and in a dress shop – places traditionally dominated by women.

Lunch
by Lotte Kramer

She came in muttering to herself.
Old age had not destroyed
Her height and bearing.

"You walked across? Such a rough day."
The waitress in her chat
Showed slight concern.

"Roast beef today and apple-tart."
The plastic turban gone
Her face was naked:

The twist and movement more revealed,
Her bones, a brittle grate, with
Beauty burnt away.

Are these the only words each day,
The only other hands
Holding a plate?

And as the radio crackled jazz
Her unheard, gutted mouth
Was never still.

> from *More New & Collected Poems* (Rockingham Press, 2015)

She has explained how writing enabled her to face up to her experiences as a child refugee from Nazi Germany:

> Reactions to my being a foreigner caused pain for a long time. During the war a girl in a laundry where I worked attacked me when her husband was killed, not aware that I was anti-Nazi. When we moved out of London to the country, the isolation brought back the time of my emigration and the childhood memories I had buried for thirty to forty years. My aim in writing about that time was to record everything. I write not only on holocaust-related themes, but also about landscapes, relationships etc. Even so, I am stereotyped as a 'holocaust poet'.

> from 'Pain into Poetry', Lotte Kramer, ARTEMISpoetry (Issue 2, May 2009), Second Light Publications.

I first read Kramer's famous poem, 'Exodus', on a London tube train. It's a poem about Nazi death camps, about any woman whose child is in danger, children escaping Germany as refugees, separated from their families. But its first stanza, 'For all mothers in anguish / Pushing out their babies / In a small basket ...', is also written for any woman with a pram, exhausted by feeding, rocking, and lack of sleep. It's only at the end of 'Exodus' that the poem becomes specific enough for a reader to relate it to a time in world history, but even then, it speaks to any refugee.

This is why 'Lunch' interests me, because, like 'Exodus', it's universal. Kramer's work is finely pitched. She paints a portrait of silence in this older woman, brittle, burned, gutted, unheard, that is tender enough, but nevertheless hints to the reader that she has isolated herself. See how 'muttering' is attached to 'old age', then 'concern' and 'naked'. The poem shows the paucity of language, and in its spareness, the reader sees the bare necessities the woman exists on, the cruelty of that limited framework of words. What do we first hear? Muttering. Her height and bearing is not celebrated, it exists as something which survived despite everything. The woman's naked face is bones and a fireplace – a metaphor of horror – and at the end of the poem although we understand she's eating, we also know that anything she might say is pointless. The poem continues to give. Who is the unknown observer, watching the woman and waitress? The first person is kept out, this is a documentary experience. This woman is so entirely isolated that even the observer is anonymous. She has no champion, she elicits only 'slight concern'. Kramer's use of speech interrupts my dream of the poem, the intensity of imagining the life of this woman through a spy camera, intimate and almost transgressive. She is also showing us the materiality of words, fitting them to the naked face.

Six
Politics and Social Engagement

Everyone has their moment of insight, discovery, a realisation that things don't have to conform to a dominant ideology. Poly Styrene singing 'Oh bondage up yours' is a memory of a time when I was beginning to think more deeply about writing and social engagement. There were few women poets on my degree curriculum but we were at least introduced to Denise Levertov, first published in the UK in 1946. Politically conscious and active, she was forever associated with the Black Mountain poets, a hit in the Poly's English department. Studying in the UK in the mid 1970s meant you experienced a homogeneous poetry scene – deeply traditional, white and male-dominated – only slightly disturbed by Linton Kwesi Johnson's *Dread Beat An' Blood* (Bogle-L'Ouverture, 1975).

In the US, however, Sonia Sanchez, Joy Harjo, Maya Angelou, Alice Walker, Nikki Giovanni, Jayne Cortez and others had followed Gwendolyn Brooks in altering the landscape. Poets wrote against war and for civil rights and wrote poems of their time, immediate and engaged. It's not that women poets weren't present in the UK, but they were marginalised. In her poem, 'The Joy of Writing', Wisława Szymborska describes poetry as 'Taking revenge against the hand of death.' A poem is an escape and an act of care. For years I regarded writing as an act of self-expression, refusing to admit I had agency as a poet, a role to express the lives of others. I believed the only valid view I could express was what I saw, however limited. I could not speak for others. Well, I can't speak for others, but I can see things differently and this is where I begin to approach the truth of social engagement, the scope of political art, its versatility, sophistication and adaptability.

'Poetry reaffirms our common humanity by revealing to us that individuals, everywhere in the world, share the same questions and feelings. Poetry is the mainstay of oral tradition and, over centuries, can communicate the innermost values of diverse cultures.' Within this statement from UNESCO (United Nations Educational, Scientific and Cultural Organisation) there are two concepts that illustrate the meaning of public poetry: our shared experience and the oral tradition.[17]

Our shared experience turns us towards poetry for weddings, funerals, births, break-ups and other life stages. These are times we need something familiar and off the shelf that'll do the job of channelling or celebrating what we feel, like Margaret Atwood's 'Variations On The Word Love' that comes up in a search for wedding poems, or Elizabeth Barrett Browning's 'Sonnets from the Portuguese 43' and Nikki Giovanni's love poem, 'Resignation'. No-one needs to analyse why we need poems at these times, it's an instinct. I don't need to analyse, either, why I've been reassured by Lucille Clifton's 'Homage to my Hips' and why young women still respond to Maya Angelou's 'Still I Rise'. Some poems are inevitably more public than others. They might not necessarily have been conceived as anthems but we send them to each other, they're anthologised, they catch a mood.

Then there's the other public role awarded to the poet herself, to maintain the oral tradition even in an era of print. When the young poet Amanda Gorman asserted, at the inauguration of US President Biden, that, 'a skinny black girl descended from slaves and raised by a single mother can dream of becoming president' she was reminding us of poetry's roots in rhetoric, the devices Plath learned from Thomas and which he'd learned from the

Welsh preachers. Poets laureate, commissioned poets, poets in residence and every variation on the theme, are working in the public sphere. The first US youth poet laureate at this event watched by millions told us: 'It's because being American is more than a pride we inherit. / It's the past we step into and how we repair it.' I love that rhyme and the way it kneads the concepts of inheritance and repair into one another like a loaf. I've always admired good rhymers because they have the wizardry to entertain, they enjoy the showiness of words and in their work they are such inventors.

The Poet as Witness

I'd argue there's another urgent element to poetry's role as defined by UNESCO and that is the choice of the poet to speak out. Poets may indeed attend the inaugurations of presidents but they're also still imprisoned – like Iranian poet Sedigeh Vasmaghi whose sentence was highlighted by PEN International in 2020. Poets from virtually every country who have spoken out against violence and repression over the centuries take this risk.

And in making a conscious choice to be a witness, like Choman Hardi and young British poet Warsan Shire, they move into a different kind of public role because of what they are writing. It's not the role satisfied by the wedding and funeral poem, by the rallying poem or the praise poem. It's a dissident's role in the broadest sense and it comes from an awareness of what isn't being heard. Shire's poem, 'Home', was widely shared online because of how it communicates the experience of refugees and immigrants. She has spoken about her need to tell the stories of people who can't tell their own, drawing on the experiences of her family and resisting the 'victim' stereotype.[18]

Poets committed to social justice, to channelling otherwise untold experiences are working in widely differing circumstances. As we know, there are writers whose words might kill them, have killed them and others, like Shire, who talk of the responsibility they feel to express untold stories. Carolyn Forché's famous prose poem, 'The Colonel', from *The Country Between Us* came out of work she was doing in El Salvador as a journalist. The poem's graphic imagery is set against a constrained, almost deadpan tone, reminiscent of a dispassionate war photographer's gaze. Forché's career has built steadily on exploring what poetry of witness means. She is the editor of two anthologies, *Against Forgetting: 20th Century Poetry of Witness* and, with Duncan Wu, *Poetry of Witness: The Tradition in English* (W. W. Norton, 1993 and 2014).

When I saw Choman Hardi read her poems from her collection *Considering the Women* (Bloodaxe Books, 2015) they reminded me of my father bringing back an American magazine that contained photos of the Sơn Mỹ Massacre in Vietnam in 1968. Can you summon a news report, the lurch in your stomach when you see an image, the need to turn away or a moment when you understand you need to act? This instinctive and visceral response underpins Hardi's collection. But the poems also address the ethical issues that arise when a poet writes about another person's experience. Monologues are drawn from her work as an academic, but she adds to this experience the impact of immersing herself in accounts of the violence and continuing trauma. This integration of lived experience and the experience of witness is one of the elements that makes Hardi's collection so authentic. When a poet has no choice it will show itself in the poems.

The poem, 'Crossing Back', which provides the collection's understated title, is about ties to home, place of birth and mother tongue but also about the responsibility of a writer to remember and give a voice to those who are silenced. Social media and mobile phones enable citizen journalists to share what they witness, and the horror we see from live feeds is graphic, almost impossible to watch. But poems keep history alive too in the care they take, and the attentiveness they offer and in their suspension of historical moments.

Poetry of witness often operates in a very different way to lyrical, detailed meditations on nature that come from a certain

English tradition reliant on microscopic burrowing down into detail that often acts as an unearthing of metaphor. However, it's impossible to generalise. In Hardi's case, 'Crossing Back' relies on its context and whoever's reading will know what's around it and what brought it into being. Even without the poems around it, the reader must make an emotional leap as the poet shows the reality of being a witness. It's a reality in which history is telescoped and lives summarised in the final word of the poem, 'slain'.

Social Engagement and Necessary Poems

One of the 1970s' most interesting writers and commentators, Audre Lorde, wrote in 1977:

> For women, then, poetry is not a luxury. It is a vital necessity of our existence. It forms the quality of the light within which we predicate our hopes and dreams toward survival and change, first made into language, then into idea, then into more tangible action.[19]

Her beautiful articulation of why any of us write also explains the motivation behind poetry of engagement as opposed to witness. We sometimes get caught up in believing that to be socially engaged demands a certain style or stance, or age, class, delivery. And that a poet's responsibility is to be as good a person as it is possible to be.

But even poetry that appears to be apolitical is making a political statement. It might be a manifesto, a lyric, you might put the 'I' in and someone else might take it out. Your poem might rhyme and another might not, yours might mix up languages and spread text across the page, be spoken or sung. What matters is what shows you, the reader, that a poem had to be written.

On the 70th Anniversary of the Warsaw Uprising
by Maria Jastrzębska

Ola says: Oh politicians, they love a dead hero.
All my life I'd wanted to build a shelter.
See, birch bark and mud plaited through
boughs of pine keep out the wind. I'd lean
my shelter of debris against a dry base
of spruce, save the lower twigs for tinder.
Those whose bodies lie under open sky,
I'd hide them. Wounded, dead, with no one
beside them, in war, in peacetime. But if I ask
Jula and Ola what poems should be about
they say: write about this day and the next,
about quarrelling then running for the bus,
about dropping your ticket, write about birches
if you must, but mostly write about kissing.

from *Small Odysseys* (Waterloo Press, 2022)

Maria Jastrzębska is a UK-based poet activist who's worked extensively within her local community, co-founding the organisation Queer Writing South and editing anthologies of work by LGBTQIA+ writers. She's also a translator and dramatist. Her writing always engages broadly with the world, reflecting her British/Polish identity and her interest in the languages we speak. Poetry that examines boundaries can't fail to be of its time in the 21st century, when it seems politicians are intent on keeping us separate. And so Jastrzębska deals with the politician archetype quickly, getting that out of the way, so she can focus on the great forests of Poland, the country's legacy of genocide, and illustrate a debate among friends about the poet's responsibility.

The poem is grounded, accessible, of its time and you can hear the discussion round a table. The poet defines the forest as a place of shelter, the poet's responsibility to shelter those who suffer alone. The shelter is described in such detail as to be tantalising, so easy to enter, built by an expert. The reader is reassured by this as well as the voice of someone whose compassion comes from doing. You can hear the small twigs breaking, the leaves underfoot, you feel the weight of bodies. Yet almost immediately, the poem turns, the narrator takes us back to the conversation we began with, reported by Ola now joined by another. The reader understands the non-sequitur at the beginning of the poem is part of a longer conversation about what art can encompass, and reminds us again of our places in the basic journeys of love and death.

But, the poem is telling us, be open, never forget about the minutiae and particularly not about what makes us human, the kiss. The historically weighted title acts as a perfect contrast to the ending, but also provides a context – like one of those great photos you see of human intimacy in the middle of chaos.

The Artists' Take

There is another way in which poetry appears in the public arena and that is when it meets visual art. In 2005 I saw an LED work by Jenny Holzer for the first time in the Gallery Lambert in Avignon. I'd become aware of Barbara Kruger and become interested in the meeting of art and text in installations, aphorisms, truisms, projections. It's an old partnership, words brought into the open air. As you explore, you begin to realise poetry has been meeting art for centuries, in calligraphy, weaving, illustrated manuscripts, tiles, ideograms. There are ancient pattern poems, altar poems, experiments with text on vellum and unusual arrangements by poets. At our best, writers and artists talk constantly over the garden wall, sharing materials and techniques to put words into the world. Perhaps in the past, these words were more likely to be sacred but arguably they take on a different sanctity now as statements about the earth, landmarks, our behaviour, relationships and history.

Links between words and image are clear in illustrated herbals, the egg of Simius of Rhodes and the thousands of Arabic poems on the walls of the Alhambra in Granada, southern Spain. Calligraphy delivers examples of language and visual art meeting in Sanskrit, as well as tanka, haiku and the poetry of many Chinese dynasties. On the African continent hieroglyphs, pictographs and other old writing systems continue to influence us; indeed, they represent the beginning of writing. The scope is enormous. So here I can only touch on the points of contact between image and word that I've drawn on.

As a rule poetry lives in the mass medium of print and privately in a reader's solitary experience. When artists place text in the public sphere words become public, sometimes ephemeral, sometimes lasting. The viewer or reader's immediate experience of the words will be in situ. I've been helped in my thinking by visual artists I know and particularly long-time collaborator Jane Fordham, who first fired the idea at me that an artist feels able to use anything as material.

In seeing words from a different perspective – not syntactically but as objects in a landscape – I came across artists who used text and writers whose text was physical. Yoko Ono, Holzer and Kruger joined walking artists Richard Long and Hamish Fulton I'd encountered in the 1990s, as well as Ian Hamilton Finlay. Holzer has used quotes from poems as well as many different types of text: truisms, public statements, warnings from a variety of sources. Her work often moves, like 'Duck and cover' a phrase on the side of a lorry driving past Capitol Hill in 2018 as part of her 'It is Guns' campaign. She's turned to the work of established writers for more recent projects, displaying poems by Wisława Szymborska on public buildings, and in 2020 included projections, moving LEDs on lorries, and phone technology to spread texts as varied as Anne Carson's *Fragments of Sappho*, *Sister Outsider* by Audre Lorde and *Citizen* by Claudia Rankin. Ever inventive, when an artist like Holzer meets the best poetry you can hear the glass smashing.[20]

Lorde herself wrote: '... there are no new ideas still waiting in the wings to save us as women, as human. There are only old and forgotten ones, new combinations, extrapolations and recognitions from within ourselves – along with the renewed courage to try them out.'[21] Kruger used her background in magazine design to create some of her most renowned provocative statements, including 'I shop therefore I am' and 'Your body is a battleground.' Her many projections have included quotes from George Orwell and provocative questions such as 'Whose values?' collaged onto a cover of *Newsweek*. These artists' use of a public, visual medium emphasises the versatility of the language we share. Here it seems right to go back to Enheduanna, and her legacy. In her final temple hymn to Nisaba, goddess of writing (translated by Betty de Shong Meador), Enheduanna describes the shrine as a 'shining house of stars bright with lapiz stones' and Nisaba as 'true woman of the pure soapwort'. The tone set by the high priestess, the first poet to write her words down, is to be grounded as well as visionary.

I remember writing tutors emphasising the importance of every word in a poem earning its place. To carve words into stone is a true test. Each line break, dot and comma must be scrutinised. And around the corner from where I live is another lesson from the dead. There's a spelling mistake on an old gravestone – separated written as seperated. It's the last stop on the graveyard tour, just before the gates.

Seven

Translation

> As a poet, translation gives me the opportunity to engage directly with poetic strategies different from my own. In attempting to recreate them in English, I am also practicing them. It is a chance to work in the "clay" of poetic language with my ego, experiences, preferences, left in the wardrobe closet.
>
> Marilyn Hacker[22]

In an interview in 2016, with Book Culture in the US, the poet Marilyn Hacker was asked how a translator chooses her languages and her reply was simple, 'you translate the languages you know.' She's translated Emmanuel Moses, Venus Khoury-Gata and Rachida Madani from French and has written about the dialogue that emerges in her own work with the poets she translates. This emphasis on the creative potential of translation is at the core of the drive to make other poets' work accessible in whatever language they are translated into. And while Hacker chooses to work with languages she knows, another approach has grown out of the middle ground opened up by poets collaborating with literal translators which broadens the options for poets who are monolingual.

The metaphors attached to the act of translating are multiple: 'the artist translator is a master potter'; 'translation is voyage'; 'the translator poet is a blatant robber'; 'a translation is an X-ray'.

These are from US poet, Willis Barnstone's *An ABC of Translating Poetry*.[23] The translation community is by necessity broad, and translation itself as much an act of creativity as writing your own poem. Poet Tara Bergin, writing in *Modern Poetry in Translation* about Ted Hughes' translations of Janos Pilinszky, describes Hughes' relationship with the literal translator, Janos Csokits, as 'a catalyst formed largely through trial and error, ignorance, imperfection, and failure; elements which are, arguably, fundamental to any creative act.'[24]

And so where does a poet start? The Stephen Spender Trust, a UK champion of translation and translators, provides a guide, *Poetry Translation for Newcomers*, written by Jamie Lee Searle, who founded the UK Emerging Translators Network.[25] Searle, who translates from Portuguese and German, writes:

> There is no right or wrong way to translate, and no such thing as one perfect translation. If you were to give the same text to ten different people, the translations they produce would be very different. What matters is being playful with language, and enjoying the process of bringing the poem into English.

Driving this belief in the diversity of translation, the Poetry Translation Centre runs workshops for poets and translators working in partnerships. Modern Poetry in Translation also runs workshops and encourages submissions of original translations for themed issues. Hacker highlights what a poet can earn from this process – a dialogue as well as a new way of working. Poet-translators also celebrate the insight a writer gains from such close attention to meaning and shape, the consequences of decisions about single words, the depth of understanding they reach when they embark on another writer's work. And for readers multiple translations must surely add layers of understanding.

MPT is one of the UK's major platforms for work in translation. In her last issue as editor, focused on Russia and the Ukraine, Sasha Dugdale wrote:

> The poetry from this region has never been more necessary to us. It provides us with a true insight into modern war and its psychological effects, measured with the finest instruments: lyric poets. With its truth-saying powers it also alerts us to the danger of imperial reach and the glorification of nationalism and military might. There is much that prophetic Russian poets can tell us about our own future.[26]

Telling, too, that subsequently MPT has turned its attention to the languages of the UK in its determination to undermine the myth that Britain only speaks English. And so translation involves constant questioning, searching and travelling.

Poets Susan Wicks and Valérie Rouzeau have spoken about their work together on Rouzeau's first UK publication, *Cold Spring in Winter (Pas Revoir)* (Arc Publications, 2009), a book-length sequence of poems about the death of Rouzeau's father, a scrap metal dealer. The collection won the Scott Moncrieff prize and was shortlisted for the Griffin Prize 2010. Rouzeau encapsulated Wicks' role as a creative partner: 'Sue is the author of *Cold Spring* whereas I wrote *Pas Revoir*. I was of little help indeed. It's a whole job of reinventing the poems across the Channel and I owe Sue Wicks more than I can say ...'. Wicks answers, 'It's the very inventiveness of what you [Valérie] do in French that makes any translator of you have to "reinvent" – and without your poems in the original, not only the translations but that whole pretext for renewed inventiveness just wouldn't be there.'[27]

Reading the dual language collections Arc has produced you can see what Rouzeau means. In a translator's preface, Wicks details some of the difficulties she faced conveying Rouzeau's use of language which she says reminded her of James Joyce, William Faulkner, Montaigne, Pascale, Boris Vian, Apollinaire and Plath. 'The whole sequence was a translator's dream, or a translator's nightmare. The first line of the first poem ('Toi mourant man au telephone pernoctera pas voir papa.') had me blinking,' Wicks writes. Her challenges in rendering Rouzeau's inventions included,

'Puns, slang, hybrids, coinages, Anglicisms, baby-talk, inversions, words which seem to belong equally to the phrase that precedes them and the one that follows ...'. For one poem she 'needed a word that was part bike and part balloon' and so had to improvise:

> I take my father's bike.
> Radiant with spokes as if set free.
> Aluminium frame, the cows take off.

> > from *Cold Spring in Winter (Pas Revoir)* by Valérie Rouzeau
> > trans. Susan Wicks (Arc Publications, 2010)

In 2021, the shortlist for the first Sarah Maguire prize for Poetry in Translation included Takako Arai, Nouri Al-Jarrah, Fawzi Karim, Kim Yi-deum, Judith Santopietro and Yang Lian – poets writing in Japanese, Arabic, Korean, Spanish and Chinese. And as the slim spines of MPT expand on my bookshelf, poets of the Maghreb, Japan, Caribbean, India, of Britain and Europe, gather at what seems like a long and constantly moving festival. At the turn of the millennium, Daniel Weissbort, then editor of MPT, wrote about the many Englishes and other languages spoken in Britain. Of course he was not the first to express this but perhaps that is another responsibility of the poet and the translator, to keep bringing ourselves back to what feeds us. An outdated desire to uphold a received English in the English ruling class and educational elite may have hidden this reality for years, but most other communities have not just retained their versatility, but celebrated and benefited from it – easily switching between dialects, registers, languages, slang, constantly creating. As the work of Wicks and Rouzeau shows, poets are always there, in the middle of it all, since we are eternally mindful of our material. And another of the many champions is poet Debjani Chatterjee, a translator from Bengali.

A Bengali Woman in Britain
by Safuran Ara (trans. Debjani Chatterjee)

A Bengali woman in Britain earns her bread,
her life is not confined by narrow limits.
Hard looks can hold no threat for her,
she is no homeless beggar or victim.
A Bengali woman in Britain does not easily surrender.
She is no still and silent statue.
Nothing startles her, no sudden noise;
she is no golden deer caught in a veil of illusion.

Though far from home, she is no straw adrift on the tide.
The scent of lemon, moonlight dancing on tamarind leaves,
music in the drizzling of Monsoon nights, grip her in nostalgia.
Even today such sweet memories have not dimmed.

A Bengali woman in Britain
has yearnings unfulfilled but her head is unbowed.
She is no wretch to crawl in anyone's dust.
Do not view her with pity, she is no beggar.

A Bengali woman in Britain
arose one dawn and flew, she soared wild on wings.
She is not insignificant, she needs no looks of sympathy,
she is no angelic being, nor some drunkard's slut.
She is no mysterious goddess, she wants no worship.

> from *Songs in Exile/Probashir Pala: A bilingual collection*
> trans. Debjani Chatterjee (Sheffield Libraries, 1999)

The title which becomes a repeated line underlines the poem's central theme – what does it mean to be displaced, whether by choice or circumstance? It's a political poem embedding a message

– 'no looks of sympathy' – into a long list of what this woman is not. The intimate nature of the poem suggests the woman in the title is the woman reading it, despite the writer's use of the third person. In fact, the use of the third person emphasises the woman's feeling of otherness, her awareness of how she is seen. She has no name, either. The other dominant device in the poem, showing someone by what they are not, serves to show the reader the stereotype, the exhausted media tropes of a woman whose multi-faceted life is endlessly reduced and confined by racism. Ara has chosen this device, perhaps, because the woman's displacement is the most overwhelming definition she has – it describes all she has left and is no longer able to take for granted. But the poet is also using this device to challenge onlookers and their range of preconceptions spanning the spectrum of racism and stereotyping. Her images range from the aesthetically beautiful to the urban. Think again, the poem asks the reader, challenge cultural ignorance, challenge stereotyping and pity. At the centre of the poem, Ara places the woman's own 'sweet memories' but they are ring-fenced, they are hers. For much of the rest of the time, the poem tells us, she is defined by strangers as anything from goddess to beggar, angel to slut. We don't need to know why she left – for now, just what she is not. Chatterjee is extensively published as a poet, children's writer and translator. Ara has co-edited several anthologies, including *Kavitanjali*, a collection of Bengali women's poetry.

If it Wasn't for Translators

Before 2020–21, year of the pandemic, if I wanted to see poets read their work live, there were some opportunities in my city but generally I'd have to travel and weigh up the cost of entry as well as the train. But Covid-19 gave us online poetry readings and global access. Some poets devote lifetimes to translating the work of others but those of us brought up speaking a globally dominant language might, in practical terms, not immediately be aware of the constant translating that goes on daily among the world's people.

Mandarin, Spanish, Hindi, Arabic, Bengali, Portuguese, Russian, Japanese, Punjabi and Swahili sit with English in the world's most spoken languages but on top of these are thousands of languages, some used by millions, others increasingly threatened, and for billions of people switching between languages is normal.

There will always be difficult times and always a need for connection. If it wasn't for translators, how would I have known about the syllabic form, lickos? I'm never going to be able to travel to south eastern Iran to listen to this "poetry of the desert" spoken by women, that in turn reminds me of landays, another form determined by a syllable count and also claimed by women.[28] Translators, whether or not they are working with a language they speak, read or know, are people I'll happily sit around a camp fire with, in awe at their ability to expand and shrink the world simultaneously, to sprinkle powder into the flames and see what happens. A poem in translation disrupts the incessant drone of English and asks us to listen for something else.

Ted Hughes said of the 1960s, when he launched *Modern Poetry In Translation*, 'One can easily understand the suddenness of the need to communicate, to exchange dreams and revelations and brainwaves, to find a shared humanity on the level of the heart.' So it was my heart that responded when I read this next poem by Wang Xiaoni, a Chinese poet whose work is available in English thanks to a number of different writers and translators. I'm in a poetry reading group and we were conscious of our ignorance of contemporary Chinese writers. I don't need to explain the impossibility of grasping a country's writing in a couple of hours. All we could do was browse. And a pair of shoes spoke to me.

At the Edge of a Field, a Pair of Shoes
by Wang Xiaoni

At the edge of a field,
a pair of shoes is neatly set,

and which old man led the frugal life of these?
Perhaps he only wanted to remain close to the earth.
—Sha, sha, sha, sha: you can hear hoeing in the field.
The eye fills with green, lush corn leaves.

The stalks are all so sturdy;
they must grow seeds of gold.
The pair of shoes is still new,
with fine close stitching.
—At the distance, somebody
is singing opera, a rough voice.

The whistle for rest peels.
A young man stands up from the field;
his countenance is set. Sturdy. No, downright handsome.
The sun is his huge earring.
—He is laughing, shouting and almost dancing.
"My precious shoes are still there."

He knocks the dust from his shoes,
looks at his muddy feet,
and puts his shoes under his arm.
The sun burns the road to glistening hot.
Pat, patta-pat, patta-pat, listen:
his bare feet shape the bronze earth!

trans. by Gordon T Osing and De-An Wu Swihart
from *At the Edge of a Field, a Pair of Shoes* (Salt Hill, 1998)

  I have no way of knowing how close this is to the original tone and vocabulary. But the poem works for me because of the way it sets up and knocks down the story of the shoes and the land. The poet makes me conscious of what this image initially suggests – the shoes belong to someone close to the land, and they must be old. The poet, listening, is overwhelmed by sounds from the field and by the mass of sweetcorn. The shoes, being part of this landscape, must then be frugal. I am reminded of fables, stories of the land and the poet builds on that sense of discovery and otherworldliness by turning the corn into seeds of gold. The shoes change now – the poet sees they're new, well made. The story isn't as it seemed and the sounds of the corn change too, into opera, but the poet keeps it real, the singer's voice is rough, untrained.

It's become a fully narrative poem with the shoes being our way into the poet's fantasy and interrogation of what she's seen. The young man becomes an archetypal figure, a worker governed by a boss's time, the whistle, and as such, he represents the truth, the everyday. This isn't the poet's truth, which began with a preconception, but a different contemporary reality focused on his relief his shoes haven't been stolen, too valuable to get dirty. His shoes move him between worlds. So the poem ends, as it started, with the pair of shoes and sound, but the sound is of him, real now, not a poet's mistaken fantasy.

What work so well for me in this poem are the sounds and the rhythm of those sounds – they are melodic and percussive, they are simple and accessible, they could be childish or sophisticated and in between them are the sounds of opera made democratically available, the human voice and a whistle. The poem is a soundscape and sounds make the rest of the poem a stage, an emotional and dramatic journey in four stanzas from the idea of the old man of the land, the image appealing to the reader's sentimentality, to that of a young man who's empowered to shape the landscape and is more like a god with his sun-earring.

Wang Xiaoni, born in Jilin in 1955, was herself an agricultural labourer during the Cultural Revolution. Her collection, *Something Crosses My Mind*, translated by Eleanor Goodman, was shortlisted for the 2015 Griffin Prize. In an interview with the Shanghai Literary Review, Goodman identifies what she admires about Xiaoni and I wasn't surprised. The poet she knows is the poet I've picked up in my scant readings of her poems online. I was somehow reassured by her portrait of a woman as observer, who has decided not to be explicit but is nevertheless intensely political.[29]

She's an ordinary woman. And you often see that in her verse. She writes from that perspective – there's a lot of buying fruits and vegetables, etc. However, I think underneath all of that is an intense political awareness.

More than anything, when Goodman reveals Wang Xiaoni is a gardener, I go back to the poem's ability to connect me with the earth and her sense of fabulous interaction that gardeners feel. I think of Olive Senior, of Sarah Maguire, of all the poet gardeners, and I hear that man banging his shoes together, I see the field of tall plants, their nuggets of sweetness.

Part Two

Writing & Working with Poems

Eight
Running a Workshop

I used to think of my working life in two parts – before and after workshops. First, I paid the rent with journalism. Life changed in 1999 when I embarked on a long residency with poetry workshops at the heart of it. And so I'm changing focus in the following chapters to look at facilitating writing for other people, while still feeding my own.

I learned how to run workshops by trying to mirror what I'd experienced. I've often been nervous, sometimes daunted and occasionally felt I'd failed miserably. But at its best, a workshop leaves me feeling exhilarated because of the ideas, lines and metaphors that have been delivered around the table, in a circle of chairs or outside in a park, on the beach, in the woods.

What Makes a Workshop?

The room, for the time a workshop lasts, is a world. The writer puts the elements in place – a room, a view, a place with history (sometimes), and a group of people. I want a workshop to make me feel I'm in the moment of a poem or story – everyone sitting at the same table, feeling excited because we'll be creating something new. For people taking part, the day is time out to stretch, concentrate on writing, so I make the tea, fill up water jugs, and get out plates and cutlery. They want to fill up pages, walk at lunchtime and come back with something to tell.

I remember my excitement being driven down the lane to the Arvon Foundation in Yorkshire and the careful feedback of tutors James Berry and Vicki Feaver. I encountered writers I'd never heard of in workshops with Matthew Sweeney. From a day at the South Bank Centre in London, I remember Liz Lochhead's generous and relaxed approach and this has become a standard I aim for.

Organising It Yourself

Most writers are invited to deliver workshops and don't have to deal with administration or publicity. I've occasionally organised a workshop myself, but juggling bookings, fees, venue and publicity takes time and is risky because people drop out at the last minute. To put on your own workshop you need public liability insurance, payment in advance with no refunds if someone cancels, a reliable venue and a good network of people to spread the word. You also need to calculate the time it takes you to organise and add that into the cost.

Themed or specialised workshops attract attention. Ask writing friends what they'd like. Decide on numbers. Find a special place to put it on – but when you're calculating what to charge, add up venue hire, your fee, travel, planning time and publicity costs. Warn participants it can only go ahead with a minimum number. Set a cut-off date so if you don't break even, you can cancel and refund.

Working for Someone Else

I've done workshops on beaches and in woods, in a stately home, a youth hostel, a touring youth bus, secure unit, Japanese garden, arboretum, school grounds, in galleries, pubs, libraries, day centres and museums. Once I heard someone say, 'Let's put Jackie in the skate park.' It didn't happen. I've been asked to suggest themes, build a workshop around specific writers or ideas and develop a session on journal writing. When someone rings or emails me, the first things I need to know are:

- When is it?
- Where?
- How long do you want?
- Who's it for?
- What's the fee?

I allow at least a day to develop new materials for a workshop, particularly if I am doing new research for a theme, or on writers I haven't covered before. I expect my fee to cover preparation as well as the time I'm delivering the workshop. When I write a series of workshops I build in time for meetings – face to face or on the phone – to share a draft plan and amend it if necessary. I want to know who's taking part and what will work for them. If it's in a school, I need to know the students' ages, if anyone has special educational needs. If it's for adults are they beginners or experienced writers?

I'm cautious if the organiser is putting on a workshop as an outreach activity – maybe a drop in. The risk is that participants have no interest in writing but the organiser thinks it might be good for the clients. Perhaps she has never put on a writing event before but has found a source of funding. So before undertaking an outreach project, I need to know if participants have been consulted, if there's a goal for the project e.g. book, recording, performance, who is responsible for the group's welfare/safety, who will be supporting me and how, that there are minimum and maximum numbers of participants and that the venue's suitable.

Well-planned outreach work combined with workshop planning can deliver life-affirming and long-reaching results.

Momentum

A good workshop has a momentum and a rhythm that keeps the creative process energetic. It has four parts: introduction, ice-breaker/lead-in, focus, wrap-up.

- After names and introductions, go quickly into an ice-breaker or easy exercise to loosen up and lead into the theme of the workshop. It can be a writing exercise you know achieves results easily.
- When people are loosened up, focus and take them inward so they can write.
- At the end of the day, everyone needs time to share work, talk or ask questions.
- In a longer workshop, the structure doesn't change but you can vary exercises, the mood and experiment.
- By the afternoon of a day-long workshop, people are writing well, are excited by their material and want to shape a piece of writing.

Keep Workshop Plans

I have a photo of a swan on a slipway and whenever I see it, I remember a room, its view and the walk we took. I couldn't remember so precisely though, what we did in the workshop and that's why I keep workshop plans.

Sometimes themes crop up again and I rework a day or afternoon I've spent hours finding materials for. Then there are the times when I'm invited back and I have to remember what I've done a year earlier. I try to stick to a workshop plan but when I veer off, because I've included too much, I make a note of what I've ditched. One of the most useful notes to make, too, is on timing. This is sometimes hard to judge and I don't like to kill an interesting discussion just in order to keep to my schedule.

Workshop plans are interesting to look back on. I have held onto certain exercises because I know they work, but after a while need to try something else. Then I forget them because they've been sidelined by new ones. When I revive an exercise, I bring something else to it and season it differently. My workshop plans show me which exercises I am over-reliant on. They keep me inventive and enquiring.

I haven't got a comprehensive record of workshops I've delivered and I regret it. Three A4 books I've glued poems and exercises into over the past decade have been my reference books and personal anthologies, constantly updated with new material. I could probably trawl through endless notebooks if I was desperate to locate a particular workshop plan, but it would take a long time. I've lost records, too, when I've upgraded computers. So now I have a workshop folder and everything goes in there.

Caution!

Everyone has a bad or difficult experience of a workshop. Some are almost a rite of passage – it's a drop-in session and no-one turns up, you're in a classroom full of teenagers who think they have a free 45 minutes and the teacher's gone off to do his marking, a care home engages you for a reminiscence project but won't turn off the TV.

But my worst experiences have been when someone has attempted to interfere with the content. Indeed, the very worst was a firm that returned my workshop plan with comments on my choice of poems. It expected learning objectives for each exercise and wanted to circulate my proposal to a steering committee. When it demanded copyright on my materials we parted company. But I kept one of the comments scribbled on my schedule: 'Here are some random thoughts after a quick read Please feel free to disregard them, since I haven't read a poem since Philip Larkin died ... I don't know how each poem illustrates your points, but my sense is that there are too many of them, and some may be a bit precious.'

Evaluation

There's a wonderful tradition at the end of a course at Tŷ Newydd or one of the Arvon centres of producing an anthology of work written during the week. Increasingly, too, organisations expect formal evaluation of a workshop, whether to please funders or fit their own procedures. After residencies I have written reports and sometimes left a collection of exercises with examples of work.

All these things mark the event and in some cases I have used the results of evaluation sheets to alter or promote future workshops. Sample evaluation sheets are simple to find and adapt. I keep to one page and no more than five questions with space for comments.

At the end of two school residencies, I put together a book of exercises for teachers. I used a simple template to summarise how I had used each exercise and as I brought them together I found I was also evaluating my work and methods:

How does this poem work?
How can it be used?
Example of poems written in response to this poem.

My favourite end-of-residency books were handmade with primary school children. We used card, handmade paper and stitched them simply. But *Boiola*, a booklet produced during a Unilever residency, reached the heady heights of the D&AD awards where it was shortlisted for a Pencil. This was a reminder for participants of exercises we'd done together and was initiated largely by the writer I was working with, John Simmons.

Nine

The Model

There are broadly two workshop paths – to generate new writing or bring writing for critical feedback. Some merge both.

Critical Feedback Model

Both writers' workshops I attend – one in London and one in Brighton – are for sharing and discussing poems. These groups have become the first place to try out a new poem or a sequence. I was invited to join both groups and I miss them badly if I can't attend.

The poets in these groups are friends, peers, trusted readers and experienced writers. I trust them to read my work closely, to be honest, to identify the weaknesses and strengths in my writing and to ask questions if they don't understand what I'm doing. When I was starting to write, I went enthusiastically to both models of workshop but soon realised that good critical feedback was harder to find. A one-off workshop of this kind relies on an experienced, energetic and organised writer to lead it. The leader/facilitator has to be fair with time and aware that some participants might be fragile. She should have a good grasp of group dynamics and be prepared to establish ground rules from the start.

Outside a closed group like the two I belong to, one of the best approaches I've come across is to look at poems without names on. The workshop leader may ask for copies in advance, or ask each participant to bring a number of copies on the day. If participants know one another, there's always a chance they will recognise one another's style, but anonymity allows people to be more objective and not influenced by a sense of loyalty. The writer leading this kind of workshop is truly a facilitator and while her name may have been the reason people signed up and handed over cash, she makes sure each piece of work has its due. The way she does it is: she ensures every poem is read aloud, there is time to re-read it silently, she encourages others to comment so her opinions are not dominant, she intervenes if a comment is offensive (although this is rare), she may attempt to sum up at the end and she offers her own views on an equal basis to the others. She may ask the poet to identify themselves immediately or wait until all the poems have been discussed.

Another variation on the model is when poems are submitted in advance for the facilitator to read and her feedback is the focus of the workshop. In this case writers are identified and while the group is less actively involved in the feedback, everyone benefits from seeing how the facilitator has approached the poems.

The structure of a critical workshop is pretty simple – the allotted time may be divided up in equal portions. Some workshop leaders ask for a volunteer to signal when time's up. It's fair and avoids long silences but this kind of limit doesn't work for longer, more experimental writing that needs time. In a day-long and sometimes even in a half-day workshop there's time for close reading and writing exercises.

Both groups I go to finish when we've said what we want. In a closed group there's no need for anonymity because part of its strength is the fact that you know one another's style, interests and approach. The group, therefore, reads its own work with in-depth knowledge and understanding and will often revisit pieces a writer brings back again and again. Most poets I know are in at least one group, many are in more than one. I value the mutual support and the deep insight a group gives me into other poets' work, take pleasure in seeing work published that I have seen in draft. In a good group, people like one another and celebrate individual styles. That might seem like an obvious statement, but I remember one that rewrote poems by committee until all individuality was edited out, another that prided itself on the viciousness of its feedback and one deferential group that almost worshipped at the feet of a powerful individual.

Change

A writing workshop can be a catalyst for social change by giving a group of people the opportunity to express themselves and feel empowered. It nurtures insight and ability: the insight needed to read carefully and critically as well as developing writer's craft. Trust between workshop participants is essential. Some writers' workshop groups have become legendary, because of their participants or for the change they initiated. Participants of long-standing workshop groups develop a deep understanding of one another's work as they witness it develop.

Masterclass

The term masterclass is so overused it's teetering into the territory of parody, but I'll give it the benefit of the doubt because if you can get it right, it works. The masterclass often follows the critical workshop model, but it doesn't have to. There are residential masterclasses that aim to extend writers through critical feedback and writing exercises. The masterclass question is less about what model it uses and more about what participants expect or how they're selected.

There seems to be a point writers reach – a first pamphlet, the manuscript of a first collection, first draft of a novel, a few stories published – when they want to be with writers at the same stage of development. I think this is because we instinctively know we can learn from one another as well as from a workshop leader. But the concept of a masterclass is being abused. I've seen it used to confer seriousness or underline the status of whoever's leading it. I've seen it used to justify a higher ticket price. It's become a marketing term.

So is it for the exceptionally gifted, the advanced, is it a performance in front of an audience? Is it defined by the skill of the tutor or by the fact it's selective? I wonder if the participatory writing masterclass that comes from a workshop model is formalising two tendencies? The first is peer grouping that so often happens among writers and artists (once called a movement, now a network) and naturally they share work, ideas and methods. This leans towards the closed critical workshop that recruits by invitation. The second is informal mentoring by a more experienced writer that happens if you're lucky or in the right place at the right time. This leans towards the writer-led workshop.

Some masterclasses are selective. Some specify a participant has to be published/submit work in advance/be invited, some focus on the skill of the workshop leader and limit numbers to justify a higher fee. At different times in my life I've found it difficult to subject work to the scrutiny of a group of strangers because the experience can be painful. I came across the 'feedback sandwich' when I began working for the Open University – positive feedback, anything negative next, end with something else that's positive.

I don't apply a formula so rigidly, but I know there's always something positive to say about a piece of writing, however flawed and I wouldn't assume that because someone's in a masterclass they're any more hardened to feedback they hear as 'bad'. But in a masterclass, you have to assume participants want an honest view.

Exercise Model

Most workshops I've been invited to run are for generating new writing. The exercise model is without doubt favoured by beginners, the one that most people identify as a writing workshop and it is infinitely flexible. For many beginners, content is key and to a degree their instincts are correct – extreme or unusual themes and ideas make poems stand out to editors and competition judges. I introduce craft, technique and form when reading the work of published poets and discussing editing.

I don't specialise in particular forms like some poets, although many of my exercises involve lists. However, I know from my own experience of attending workshops that writing under pressure of time often produces poems that wouldn't otherwise have been written.

I am always impressed by what people can write in say, 10 minutes and the reason this kind of workshop is popular is probably because many of us need a different kind of approach from time to time, a starting point or another perspective. A writer has to be inventive and a workshop is another way of filling the well that we draw on all the time.

There are exercises at the end of this book that I've used in workshops but there are many other sources of ideas for writers who are beginning to run workshops. Most writers don't mind if you use their exercises – but credit them. When you do that, you're acknowledging the amazing resource that exists – much of it not collected or written down.

People attend this kind of workshop for many reasons and it's a very adaptable model. I've used the same template with extremely different groups of people and all ages. But what I think is most appealing about turning up at a workshop and being given exercises to do is that it takes the anxiety away from starting. I try and give people an insight into what feeds my own writing – a mixture of ideas, reading, quiet, trying out words and phrases.

Above my own writing desk is a quote from the Chinese text, *Chuang Tzŭ*, 'The hearing that is in the ears is one thing. The hearing of the understanding is another. The whole being must listen.' I select exercises to illustrate different aspects of writing and when I am given a particular goal or goals for a workshop, tailor exercises to suit those aims.

Ten

Planning

Preserve workshop plans. I have learned from mine how to fine-tune workshops, how a different order of exercises alters the dynamics of an afternoon or a day. I know which exercises are guaranteed to bring results, which are riskier. When I look at the plan of a day I know went well, I feel more confident about adding in an exercise I haven't tried before. These plans are the tools of my trade.

45 minutes

Short workshops work well if there's a theme and they move fast.

- **Introduction.** Read a poem that establishes an atmosphere or relates to a theme you want to write about. Five minutes.
- **Loosen up.** Free writing. Read a poem to show a way in. Hand out objects or postcards. 10 minutes.
- **Focus.** Read another poem that's a simple model for a second piece they can share. Guided writing, line-by-line or section-by-section. 10 minutes.
- **Share work/discussion.** 20 minutes.

Half-day

Here is a plan for a teacher's workshop of two and a half hours. I was asked to help a group of teachers from a number of schools write about myth so back in the classroom with pupils they could make up stories about a local pond.

- **2pm**: Introductions. Brainstorm myths. In pairs list myths. Share.
- **2.20–2.30**: Ice-breaker writing exercise.
- **2.30–3.30**: Four 10-minute writing exercises, done fast. Alternate who reads back.
- **3.30–3.45**: BREAK
- **3.45–4.15**: Focus on theme, develop from different angles. Three exercises. Voluntary sharing with group.
- **4.15–5.15**: Final exercise of 15 minutes. Everyone reads.
- **5.15–5.30**: Questions, summing up.

A half-day workshop needs to be fast paced and energetic. The mood will be workmanlike because everyone – you and the people taking part – are fitting this in around the day's other demands. The ice-breaker here is crucial – you have to shift people into the workshop world fast so you can make the most of the time. You need to keep an eye on your schedule, too, in a shorter workshop. I'm often tempted to move away from what I've planned. I might ditch an exercise and allow more time for something else. Sometimes this works, but not always. A workshop of this length is tightly knitted together: be very cautious about unpicking your hard work. Keep to your timings, but if you start late, ask if you can make it up at the end. If you stray for other reasons, give yourself time to think about the impact of changing your plan on the spot.

Full Day

A day accommodates changes of pace, variety, socialising, longer periods of writing and drafting. When you are working with 15 or so people over the course of a day a group forms. The workshop facilitator, or leader, whatever you call yourself, needs to be sensitive to the nature of the day and choreograph it in a number of ways. In the morning, the pace can be fast – see it as an opportunity to generate a lot of material with fast-moving exercises, offer variety and move between reading work by other writers and sparky, useful, thought-provoking activities. People often attend day-long workshops to kick-start new material and work with new ideas, hoping to leave with at least a couple of new pieces in their notebooks. Sometimes people need a walk and break from the group at lunch, but make it possible for everyone to eat together if they want. Leave books around for people to browse.

As the day wears on, everyone will have at least one piece of writing that excites them. In the afternoon, you can scale down the pace and number of exercises to allow longer periods of more focused writing. Allow more time in the afternoon for feedback as writers read their work. How you and the group manage the end of the day is particularly important. Allow enough time for a group reading, questions and discussion – although this might happen socially.

This plan shows that there's a lot of material to prepare and think about for a day's workshop. It was designed to show how poets use ideas, devices and concepts to generate original material. I wanted the workshop to demystify writing and celebrate the poets whose work I used as models for their ingenuity and technique.

A Full Day Workshop Timetable 11am–4pm:

- **11–11.15**: Introductions.
- **11.15–11.30**: Icebreaker – exercise 1.
- **11.30–11.45**: Exercise 2.

- 11.45– 2.30 : Exercise 3 & 4 showing how poets use ideas to start poems.
- 12.30–12.45: Exercise 5 – making the abstract concrete.
- 12.45–1.30: LUNCH
- 1.30–2.15: Exercise 6, 7, 8 – three devices used by poets to underpin individual poems or sequences.
- 2.15–3: Develop one piece.
- 3–3.15: TEA
- 3.15–4: Group reading of work and discussion.

Zoom Time

The Zoom workshop, with relatively few hiccups, took poetry directly into peoples' homes when none of us could meet in 2020 and 2021. This reach and accessibility is likely to mean that, in future, organisations will be much more confident in offering a mix of online and face-to-face workshops. Since 2020 I have run two 16-week series of workshops, occasional workshops, and a reading group using online platforms. What did I learn?

- If you haven't run a Zoom workshop, take part in at least one short and one long one to get a feel for them.
- Regardless of how tech literate you are, get someone from the organisation that's paying you to handle the tech side e.g. letting people in (especially latecomers), dealing with chat, organising break-out rooms, and muting the group to minimise feedback.
- Screen time's far more exhausting than real time and I hadn't realised how much I relied on 'reading a room' through body language and feel of the air.

- Have workshop materials on paper as well as on screen – it's easy to lose them.

- Have a list of participants printed out and check names against what's on screen.

- Decide before the workshop whether you'll later distribute materials you've used.

- Not everyone can afford good Wi-Fi, a laptop or a desktop computer. Online-only workshops will exclude people in poverty.

- Tablets and headphones are temperamental.

- Shared screens or a single large screen in a room are okay for participants visually, but unreliable for discussion.

- If you're using a laptop, lift the screen up from desk height so you're properly framed and check your background. Will it offend anyone?

- Be as close as possible to the Wi-Fi hub. If anyone else is at home, ban them from entering the room, gaming or streaming while you're working.

- Keep the cat out and turn your phone to silent.

Two Days to a Week

Now you have time to introduce a range of approaches to writing, try different styles. There's time for independent working and, in a residential setting, opportunity for one-to-one discussions. Many emerging writers have spent time at Arvon and its Welsh equivalent Tŷ Newydd and many established writers teach there. The Arvon/Tŷ Newydd model of a week's residential course with two tutors and one visiting reader is held up as an ideal for immersing students in writing exercises and experiments. The centres are in beautiful rural settings, all have libraries and students live as a group, sharing the cooking as well as their work. Over the week, students will be given writing exercises with the tutors, feedback, share work and read the work of others.

A Plan for a Tŷ Newydd School Week

Monday Students and tutors arrive
8pm: Introductions, icebreaker, writing exercise

Tuesday 9–1pm: Writing exercises, with break
1–2: LUNCH
2–5: One-to-one sessions, individual writing
8pm: Tutors read work

Wednesday 9–1pm: Writing exercises, with break
1–2: LUNCH
2–5: One-to-one sessions, individual writing
8pm: Guest reader

Thursday 9–1pm: Writing exercises, with break
1–2: LUNCH
2–5: One-to-one sessions, individual writing
8pm: Students choose favourite writers to share

Friday 9–1pm: Writing exercises with break
1–2: LUNCH
2–6: Students prepare anthology of work
8pm: Students read work from anthology

Saturday Depart

Every morning there is enormous potential for writing exercises to cover a lot of ground. Tutors cover different areas, depending on the nature of the course. But students will, generally, be participating in about 14 hours of workshops and potentially four one-to-one sessions with tutors, as well as at least 12 hours of individual writing time. Generally, the format for schools courses is the same as for the adult courses.

Residential courses, whether in the UK and increasingly overseas, are expensive to attend, but always life-changing. Often students are at a critical point – experiencing relationship break-ups, a change of job, retirement – and their writing often reflects this. A tutor needs to be sensitive to the emotional charge that develops during the week and the significance of the course to each individual. But writers are often invited to visit a school and this kind of short residency involves equally careful planning. When I worked in Cornwall at a primary school for three days, I centred my planning on a first day visiting a beach where we took notes, made observations and filled notebooks with material that informed work back in the school for the second and third days.

We filled plastic bags with stones, shells, driftwood and made notes for a poem about a walk. We made lists of metaphors and in the afternoon of the first day, sat in a circle to make notes about gulls and fish that they'd use later. I related each activity on the beach to the two days back at school and ensured activities in the classroom would make sense of what I was asking them to collect, observe and note. Incorporating a day for amassing material like this gives children a valuable insight into the writing process.

A Course or Series

This is an opportunity to build up a group's repertoire and introduce different aspects of writing through linked workshops but which has more the flavour of a taught course. For this course in Uckfield, East Sussex, I brought in a fiction writer for four of the sessions. Each lasted three hours so could be structured pretty much like a half-day workshop.

15 Jan: The basics of plot for short story, with Sheila Alcock

22 Jan: Using the senses

29 Jan: People from our pasts, with Sheila Alcock

5 Feb: Unlocking memory

12 Feb: Writing a short story, with Sheila Alcock

19 Feb: Writing autobiography

26 Feb: Writing poetry

5 March: Editing

12 March: Sharing work

A writer may be asked to develop a themed course lasting a number of weeks. Do not underestimate the time this will take and check what you are being paid for your planning time. Developing a course enables you to expand your choice of writing exercises and provide a good range of different approaches to that theme.

A Residency

I define an artist residency as one that lasts at least a month – although there are intensive shorter placements. Mostly, the term residency suggests a relationship with a place or people and often focuses on creative development. Thankfully, I've never planned a residency alone. What has varied between residencies is how much has been organised in advance but I'm reassured by a framework because it enables me to focus on the reason for the residency rather than being in a state of flux and anxiety about next week.

During my residency at Unilever with Lever Fabergé I was asked to sketch out a workshop schedule for the entire six months. During my residency in 1999 for the Poetry Society Poetry Places scheme, I worked in the Surrey Hills Area of Outstanding

Natural Beauty and was based in council offices in Dorking with the AONB team. While I planned some of the residency on the job, I had regular working days and agreed tasks for each week as well as an overall objective. It worked like a short-term, part-time contract and this residency started a decade of employment that grew from poetry.

For Surrey's millennium project, the 'Sea of Dreams', two painters, the public and I had to produce 1,000 banners with poems on and record more poems for a spectacular installation at the Surrey County Show. Later in 2000 I spent several weeks on a youth bus in a Sussex village, working with a filmmaker to document the experiences of settled travellers. For both these residencies, project managers did most of the planning – consulting me on dates and times. So they had pre-agreed outcomes and boundaries where I slotted into a project that had a much wider remit.

Every residency has a long-term effect, is unique and in that respect each one has taught me something new, the difficult ones in particular. Fortunately the difficult ones are rare, but I was nearly burned out by two terms in 2006 working at a Sussex primary school for a government learning programme funded by Arts Council England. I was exploring the ethos of a poetry workshop and whether teachers could apply small group techniques in the classroom with years five and six. In the background was a focus on gifted and talented children and improving SATS results – although these issues seemed to be more important for the many forms that had to be filled in and I was adamant I wouldn't engage with SATS.

Despite detailed planning and pre-meetings with the school and a programme coordinator, teachers were never fully committed and I was left more or less to my own devices. It was an unfriendly place and I was squeezed into a cookery room for the workshops. The head never got my name right, teachers had conflicting agendas and the residency was changed after I was taken on. Most seriously, though, I wasn't briefed on the children in my groups who had behavioural problems – indeed an off-the-cuff remark suggested the school had used the residency as an opportunity to transfer some of the more disruptive children out of the classroom. The school was an inward looking, closed community, suspicious of outsiders.

In my final report I concluded too many people had been involved in planning and organisation. Bureaucracy interfered, communication was too formal and worked against ideas developing. The reasons for some decisions were unclear and there were hidden agendas. I pointed out that cover for teachers should have been organised so they could be involved properly and asked: 'What is the point of working with artists if you do not use them to help develop a project – if the rules and boundaries for discussion are either so tightly drawn or unclear that collaboration is impossible?'

What made the residency bearable was the time I spent with children in the workshops. The work they produced was consistently surprising and it got better by the week. Their focus enabled me to keep the often contradictory and simplistic adult demands at bay. I learned to my cost, however, the importance of support in a residency. I finished those two terms feeling drained and marginalised. One of the questions that cogged that residency was who can I talk to? This isn't just a problem for a writer – anyone working freelance has to offload. But I was nervous of talking about concerns or insecurities in most places I've worked – worried I'd be seen as weak or incompetent or unreliable.

Now I've talked more to other writers and artists about residencies and the insecurities it can raise, I know to pick up the phone to a colleague who's probably experienced something similar. Now, too, in certain circumstances, I'd get some kind of supervision written into the residency. But perhaps I needed to go through a difficult one to appreciate the many benefits of a good residency: new people and relationships, a new workspace, secure income and a chance to develop ideas.

Eleven

Developing Workshop Materials

I develop materials for workshops to fit a purpose, sometimes because I've become bored with exercises, often because I've come across a poem that has a brilliant title or explores a striking idea. I usually write alongside people attending workshops and for that reason the exercises that follow are interchangeable – they are as likely to generate your own writing as that of others.

Inventing Exercises

I began facilitating workshops in The Caxton Arms pub in Brighton when Eva Salzman, Don Paterson and I ran Brighton Poets. We organised readings and poetry workshops followed – some with invited writers, some led by us. To start with I used exercises other people developed and published. Sandy Brownjohn's *Does it Have to Rhyme? Teaching Children to Write* (Hodder and Stoughton, 1980) was indispensable. There wasn't a lot of material on creative writing at the end of the 1980s and start of the 1990s until Peter Sansom's *Writing Poems* was published (Bloodaxe Books, 1994).

During my year's residency in the Surrey Hills I began to develop a range of exercises and it was here a number of different paths opened up. The first was being introduced to the artist Walter Bailey, whose work was used for branding the Surrey Hills. When I was commissioned to write a poem in response to one of his magnificent scorched and chainsaw-sculpted oaks it introduced me to the idea of collaborations with other visual artists. The Surrey residency also introduced me to the idea that farmers, National Trust wardens and planners might be interested in writing workshops and it led to me taking part in an environmental education programme.

So material comes out of many different situations but exercises I developed for Surrey children were straightforward and easily adaptable. I hid strips of paper under rocks, by paths, in trees, for example, and asked children to hunt for them. They had to use the line on the paper as their title: 'What the tree said to me', 'What the path told me', and so on. I used several broad approaches:

- ideas that would help respond to the setting
- finding a poem model that could be adapted
- using themes

Set Your Own Boundaries

Be clear about what you want to do with a workshop, identify its unique quality before you start generating detailed activities.

- A workshop can be pitched in many different ways, by theme like the city, family.
- Stylistic – explore the sonnet, long poem or haiku.
- You could use a single writer's work.
- Base it on ideas of, say, Egyptian amulets to open up writing.
- Make it event-based, using local history, anniversaries, festivals.

- Base it on an exhibition.
- You might have to focus ideas on one group or goal.
- There might be an agreed outcome like an anthology, or a performance.

Collect Poems

David Kendall, a literature development officer, asked me to do a year's residency at Treloar College in Alton, Hampshire, funded by the Roald Dahl Foundation. It's a residential school and college for young people with physical disabilities. I had to find models that would work as collaborative group poems as well as individual pieces. As the year progressed, I built up a significant body of exercises that I recorded for teachers with explanations of how I'd used them and examples of young people's work as a legacy. Almost all the poems came from poetry anthologies in the college library. The Treloar experience taught me to be always on the lookout for poems that could be reproduced, structurally, with different content. I kept scrapbooks and honed exercises each time I used them. I had two books – poems for children, others for adults, but the most successful poems worked with all ages. I used work by writers I love, but I also kept an eye out for poems that suggest or fit into themes. As I tried to understand what was at the heart of a good exercise I concluded that it's often the most simple concept.

Some poems lend themselves to being models either because of their title, their first line or central idea: poems like Margaret Atwood's 'This is a photograph of me', Pablo Neruda's collections *Odes to Common Things* or *The Book of Questions*, Etheridge Knight's, 'The Idea of Ancestry' and Maurice Kenny's 'They tell me I am lost' as well as Walt Whitman's 'Song of Myself'.

When I was running workshops regularly I needed to keep refreshing the exercises to keep myself alert. It's important to be surprised by the writing that people produce and when I use an exercise too often, I find myself hearing not just what comes out of that day, but the results of other workshops too. When I take along a new exercise, I feel that we are all exploring the potential of the poem it is based on. Poets are inventors and virtually every new collection that's published contains a poem worth sharing. There's another pleasure that comes from collecting poems and sharing them – reading them aloud. Sometimes I read a poem, often I ask someone to volunteer. When, nowadays, do we get a chance to read a poem aloud to others? And yet when I read a poem aloud, I am more in tune with the rhythm, the sounds, the line breaks and its pace. By reading a poem aloud, I am closer to it and begin to feel it is part of me. The more poems I collect, the more I am learning.

Themes

Working with themes is rather like browsing an encyclopaedia, there's so much choice. A big idea like the city narrows down to churches, street names or a specific area. The task is to find poems that fit and suggest different ways in for the writers you're working with. Artists' installations always suggest themes and poets' collections are often themed – think of Grace Nichols' *The Fat Black Woman's Poems* and Pascale Petit's *What the Water Gave Me: Poems after Frieda Kahlo*. Some of American poet Marilyn Hacker's work addresses AIDS, illness and death, while early work by Vicki Feaver uses myths and much of Jackie Kay's work explores identity. Ruth Padel used the life of her ancestor Charles Darwin as the inspiration for the collection, *Darwin – A Life in Poems*.

So basing a workshop on a theme gives me another opportunity to look for new material and refresh exercises. I use anthologies and increasingly websites allowing poems to be legitimately downloaded, including the Academy of American Poets, Poetry Foundation, Poetry International and NYU School of Medicine's Literature, Arts and Medicine Database. It is essential to observe copyright rules.

Props and Postcards

When I was a child I collected postcards and china horses. They went in one of my father's loft clear-outs but my obsession with postcards was revived when I began running workshops. At every museum and gallery I visited, every time there was a sale in a bookshop, I bought postcards. I have boxes on top of my wardrobe marked 'portraits', 'animals', 'objects', 'landscapes', 'people'. The most-used cards have softer corners and pen marks on. I know some of them so well, I feel I should retire them.

Postcards are an effective way to get people writing and I've found that matching them with a poem model works even better. I use them in two broad ways. One taps a writer into a model or a theme. The other engages her in concentrated looking and pure description – ekphrasis. Later the writer will take her own direction, break away from the prompt and turn the writing into something that doesn't need anything but itself. I learned not to give anyone the choice of a card – I hand them out as they come out of the folder. I prepare them in advance, I know how many people are taking part, I know what exercises I'm going to do and I know what I want the postcard to do – give someone a reason to write, something to look hard at, a point of stillness when there is nothing to worry about but the image and the words that it will release. I use postcards to help with poem models on animals, on identity, reincarnation (after an exercise by Sandy Brownjohn), on art and on place. Postcards are useful for inventing similes and metaphors as well as monologues. There are so many poems, classical and modern, that take an image as inspiration, from Homer's description of the shield of Achilles in *The Iliad* to the books of poems inspired by work in the Tate produced by Paul Durcan. Deryn Rees-Jones' powerful sequence, 'Dogwoman' in *Burying the Wren* is inspired by artist Paula Rego. I've teamed postcards with poems by Moniza Alvi and Carol Ann Duffy.

When the Sussex Arts Club existed in Brighton, it was one of the venues used by Brighton Poets. We put on readings and workshops in a small upstairs room as well as the ballroom with its cloud-painted ceiling. Craig Raine read there, Christopher Reid, Jackie Kay, Ciaran Carson and the late Michael Donaghy. In 1996, eight years before his sudden death, Michael ran a workshop I attended and he used random objects to kickstart our writing. He handed me a small snow dome with flamenco dancers inside and the poem it produced was based on a memory of my aunt visiting Spain during Franco's dictatorship. So every time I use random objects in a writing workshop, I mentally thank him for the idea. Its random, yet intimate quality turns a small object on loan into the gift of a poem.

My bag of props contains a Spiderman figure, gifts from Christmas crackers like a miniature tape-measure, things I've put in drawers because I don't want to throw them away like a dice, a marble, odd earrings, and an old bunch of keys. I have Lego, a brass cat, a stone with a hole in and a lump of crystal. The prop works like the postcard, but with the added benefit that you hold it in your hand and its textures prompt you, too. Often a prop opens up a memory that the writer wouldn't otherwise have arrived at. I keep my props in a small bag I made sitting round a fire. It's half a trouser leg embroidered with beads. Sometimes I use it as a lucky dip, so workshop participants choose without looking. Sometimes I hand objects out randomly. The brief is simple – write whatever it provokes. If you feel blank, describe it until something else happens and it invariably does. Michael's wise instruction was to meditate on the object, an instruction that eventually led me to Vasko Popa's astonishing sequence, 'The quartz pebble' in his *Selected Poems* (Penguin, 1969).

Smells

Later I developed the idea of handing people smells stored in 35mm film canisters. I put vinegar, coffee, oil, jam – anything that retained its smell – into these containers and asked people to sniff them, then write spontaneously. You might not have such easy access to film canisters in these digital days but individual take-away ketchup and mayo containers might do. This is a hard exercise to do but there is a variation on it. Start by reading the poem 'Soap Suds' by Louis MacNeice and ask people to write a list of 10 brand names from childhood that they associate with a particular smell. The first few will be easy, but then it becomes harder. As they become more difficult to find, you have to search the rooms of childhood, the kitchen, a garage, go to the bathroom and parents' room, a cellar. If you can't remember a name, write a phrase that reminds you, imagine yourself in a shop with your mother. Once you've completed the list, chose one name and start off a piece of writing about your life at that time and the people in it. There will be at least one strong memory associated with the brand, it may be of a person or people or of a place. Describe physical details: these will help you recall more. I've never forgotten a woman who wrote about engine fuel. She hadn't thought about it for years, but as she wrote she remembered the brand of fuel she associated with learning to fly a light aircraft. And that reminded her of her husband.

The writer Diane Ackerman's book, *The Natural History of the Senses* (Vintage Books, 1991), mixes passages from novels, quotes and facts with history and science. It's invaluable background reading. I was working with perfumiers when I understood how difficult it is to describe a scent. Ackerman's was the first book I found that attempts an informative and accessible review of sensory experience for those of us who aren't scientists.

Workshop Basics

- Write by hand with pen, pencil and paper. Ted Hughes, in an interview with *The Paris Review* observed, 'When you sit with your pen, every year of your life is right there, wired into the communication between your brain and your writing hand.'[30]

- Hear a piece of work by everyone. If someone doesn't

want to read aloud first time round, I suggest they do for the next exercise. I offer to read for someone too if they are really anxious.

- No phones, no laptops.
- Establish the importance of feedback. At the start suggest participants make notes of what they like, what could be improved before anyone begins to speak.

Why Write by Hand and Not on an iPad or Phone?

For years I've been aware of the different way my mind works when I'm handwriting and typing, particularly on a computer keyboard (rather than a manual typewriter). There's a different connection between my hand and brain when I'm holding a pen. Well, that's what I thought it was about. As if the rounder, more organic action of writing, the different pressure I put the pen under, the way it feels on the page, even its taste and texture, the smell of ink, might have something to do with this. A keyboard's brilliant for transferring ideas, for editing, but my best ideas come in lead or ink. Actually, often my best ideas come when I'm not writing at all, but walking, swimming, jogging. However, back to handwriting. I've always kept an eye out for comments on this. Hughes' theory that with a pen, you are 'wired into' the link between brain and hand has since been shown in many more modern studies into writing and drawing. Having said this, there are often good reasons for people to type and you must find what method works best for you.

Why I Use Models

Almost all the exercises I develop are based on a writer using the structure of another writer's poem, or the idea, or the title. I do this because taking away the fear of 'how do I start?' and 'what should it look like?' enables people to write more freely. There are many stages in a writer's development. For some, the initial discovery process is long, for others it's quicker. Poetry is an art form without mass interest, large financial rewards or fame. So people write poetry because they are driven to, because they believe in its power and want to improve.

Children are experts at seeing the world differently but too often believe their vision is the wrong one. I don't remember writing poems at school. We wrote stories. I remember proudly showing one to my mother. She read it and then told me off for plagiarism. I don't know whom I stole the idea from and didn't know how to defend myself then. But I look back and understand. I knew instinctively that the way to learn was to copy, to take apart and put back together again. Just as children do all the time with objects. I've learned to write through reading, trying new models, experimenting. I use models because they show us how something works, how we can create a world in a poem, how a poem does not need any other reference points. It is an end in itself, it does not have to justify itself, it does not need explaining. A poem can take moments or weeks to write, a minute or so to read but can stay with you for years. In experiencing how a poem is put together, you learn the pleasure of writing words that make music and pictures. You learn that with words you can give voice to your imagination, excite and frighten yourself, make anything happen. A model, too, is evidence of the conversation all writers have with other writers.

Some models are simple – I come across a title like Vicki Feaver's 'The Book of Blood'. I read the poem several times, I read it aloud and take it apart. I ask what she's doing, how the poem is built, how it progresses, why it makes such an impact on me. Often I will use a poem as a model because I want other people to appreciate the poem, to get into it by seeing its mechanics as well as hearing or reading it on a page. The same happened when I read Penelope Shuttle's poem, 'Inventing' in her collection, *Redgrove's Wife*. The poem is a list and these are always good for exercises, but by identifying the components of the list and how to explain them in a workshop, the complexity of thought in the poem emerges. The poet Selima Hill is another writer whose work I've turned to for models because she is so inventive. She works with ideas and makes them solid. Her titles are tantalising, her images are surreal and original. I've used many of her poems in workshops, particularly 'Being Fifty', 'Being a Grandmother', 'Portrait of my lover as a spoon'. I am drawn to these poets because of their boldness, which signals to all of us as writers to stretch, go beyond what we know and enjoy the feeling of daring. This is my key to running workshops – sharing that pleasure as well as understanding the mechanics of the craft.

Twelve

Working in Schools and Colleges

One of my earliest memories of primary school at the end of the 1950s was of music, the school band, where each of us had a chance to play an instrument, however badly. I want children and young people to feel the same excitement about the sounds words can make. The word literacy fills me with horror – it turns imagination into jargon.

Primary Schools

If you are asked to run workshops for very young pupils, it's likely some will struggle to write. Group poems are a way to involve all the students and show them how the model you're using works. Once you've done a group poem or had a whole group discussion, you can set individual tasks. Very young pupils respond well to exercises based on simple models with a lot of repetition, where single words change, or models that don't demand advanced vocabulary. The success of an exercise is in how you pitch it, break it down and make it work so each student can approach it with a different level of vocabulary and confidence and still see results. Young children often assume, too, that poems have to rhyme. Often I don't describe what we're doing as poetry until much later.

Whenever possible, take the chance to work outside. Moving away from the classroom shifts everyone's preconceptions about what you're doing and there's much more to look at.

One of the reasons I often use poems perceived to be for adults even with young children is that I am interested in their capacity to think differently. There are some great poems written for children, but there are also some dreadful, one-dimensional collections and anthologies of simplistic, slapstick rhymes that to me have little to do with poetry or what I believe to be at the heart of a great poem – a new way of seeing. I also believe that children have the right to hear good quality poetry that comes from a love of language and deeper emotion than just easy humour.

This was brought home to me when I was working at a school with groups of eight and nine-year-olds. Some of them spoke English as an additional language and were not confident writers. I took a risk and decided to use Ted Hughes' poem 'Lineage' from *Crow: From the Life and the Songs of the Crow* (Faber, 1970). Hughes described crow as 'God's nightmare' and his own masterpiece. The language is searing, the ideas complex, the words simple and I chose it for what it shows us about the alchemy of placing two words together, or above and below each other, how ideas accumulate and how a narrative can be short and devastating. The exercise was simple. I read the poem and guided them through with basic instructions about how to use his structure, his repeated phrase 'Who begat' and substitute their own words. I asked each of them to chose an animal as important to them as the crow was at that time to Hughes. My instructions were:

- think of a sound associated with the animal
- food
- a part of the animal's body
- a feeling the animal might create in us
- another part of the animal always associated with it
- a colour suggested by the animal (not the colour of the animal)

- a musical instrument it suggests
- a word that conveys what the animal represents
- another word suggested by the animal, to be repeated as Hughes does
- substitute their animal for crow in Hughes' line 'who begat Crow'
- write two or three lines that give us a picture of it
- write a final line that shows its beginnings.

The results were stunning and gave me confidence to use other poets like Neruda in workshops with children.

Secondary Schools

In secondary schools students are open, versatile and keen. Unless you've been asked in to work with a particularly disengaged group, your visit's a novelty (although once I discovered, to my horror, a group of students had to miss football to attend a workshop). I like to know if students sign up for a workshop or are selected by teachers. Sometimes a class is split and I have half before break, half after. When this happens I ask the first half to keep what we've done under wraps – generally I think they comply. All the principles of running a workshop with adults apply. Establish at the start some guidelines on feedback – one person speaks at a time, feedback should be constructive and point out positive and negative elements in the work, no-one apologises before reading their work aloud, there's no right or wrong way to write. Young people in secondary school are sophisticated thinkers but often self-conscious and shy. In a mixed group, I've noticed they're often reluctant to volunteer to read aloud, so to save time, I suggest a 'read around' of each exercise, or alternate sharing work from different tables.

Once, at a particularly touchy school, I was asked to go through the material I planned to use beforehand because the teacher was concerned about highly religious parents. Normally, though, I am less worried about the content of the writing I take along, more about support in the workshop. It is not my role to keep discipline during a workshop, so if discipline is likely to be a problem, the school or college needs to provide another adult. I am delighted if there are other teachers or assistants around who want to participate – but they have to write and read out, like everyone else.

The results of workshops in secondary schools are often extraordinary because teenagers are reading and writing so much more than at primary school. Of course, there are often one or two who are disaffected, too chatty, challenging. But in my experience, they may also turn out to be the most interesting writers. If in doubt in a secondary school I'll opt for more difficult exercises – teenagers are quick thinkers, adaptable and generally in the mood for risk.

Special Educational Needs

Schools seem to identify gifted and talented students in various ways and may include students who have difficulties writing but who are very imaginative. They will be more confident working alone, though, and quick to grasp the idea of an exercise. When I ran Saturday workshops for West Sussex County Council's gifted and talented scheme, I was constantly surprised by the work that students as young as seven and eight could turn out. Your visit is an opportunity for these young people to stretch – they will respond to challenge. However, you won't necessarily have information about children with special educational needs before a workshop: perhaps a cover teacher doesn't know them, perhaps they're too busy.

In one school a young boy in my group had just arrived from France. Before that he was in Angola. He spoke only Portuguese and was living in a refuge. Only a teaching assistant could communicate with him – he was angry and distressed. At break I spoke to the assistant and we agreed, against the teacher's wishes, that he should write in Portuguese. He engaged and calmed down. In another school, I asked a nine-year-old boy who'd slid into the room on his knees and came to a halt under the table to go outside and walk in properly. He left the room and disappeared. Eventually a teacher walked by with him and said she'd keep him with her. At break we talked – she asked me if I'd been 'told about him'. I hadn't – but he had profound emotional problems that all related to being excluded. I should have been told – I wouldn't have asked him to leave the room.

Two case studies identify some of the issues that cropped up when I was working with different groups of young people. I have worked with children classed as gifted and talented and young people with restricted language.

Case Study: West Sussex County Council Gifted and Talented Scheme

For several years I ran full-day Saturday workshops at teachers' centres in West Sussex as part of the local authority's scheme to support gifted and talented students in primary and secondary schools. The youngest were seven, the oldest 15 and students came from different schools so they did not know one another. For workshops with younger pupils, I worked with an assistant. In the mornings we wrote and after lunch prepared a poem for a performance to parents. The continuity of these workshops allowed me to try out new exercises. The poems that invariably got results were those based on a simple form using sophisticated ideas and metaphor. I found the imaginations of these children and young people were limitless, they needed opportunities to generate metaphors and similes and they loved the freedom of thought that poetry offers.

My focus was to offer them as many different ways of writing a poem as was possible in a day, to show them variety by listening to one another's work and develop the ability to offer feedback.

Some of the most successful starting points were Carol Ann Duffy's 'The Bridge of Toys', Ted Hughes' 'Cows', Roger McGough's 'The Sound Collector', George MacKay Brown's 'The Guardians', extracts from Pablo Neruda's *The Book of Questions*, 'This is a Photograph of Me' by Margaret Atwood, 'Fairy Tale' by Miroslav Holub, 'I am Taliesin' translated by Ifor Williams, 'Words' by Alastair Reid, and Dionne Brand's 'Morning'. I used the ideas and extracts from Carl Sandburg's 'Wilderness'. Often I used a poem model with a postcard or an object.

An important feature of the day was the performance to parents. Why? Poems are written to be spoken and I wanted the children and young people taking part to feel proud of their work, to project their poems and enjoy listening to one another's achievements.

Case Study: Treloar College, Alton

I began my residency at Treloar College with a workshop for tutors and attended the college on Tuesdays during winter and spring terms to work with access and performing arts students. The body of the residency culminated in arts week, when access students performed work they produced during workshops. It was a first for each of them. My involvement with performing arts students ended with the production of their play in June. On top of these sessions, I ran a workshop for Alton College students, open Saturday workshops for students and a training session for staff at the end of the residency, when I distributed a resource pack of exercises I had used. David Kendall was a co-tutor for Saturday workshops. In all, my residency totalled 16 days. David initiated the residency with ongoing support from the manager of the Learning Resource Centre.

It was a challenge for me to work with access students who had extremely limited or non-existent speech, since it was the first time I had any regular contact with young people with these kinds of learning disabilities. Some students used language aids, most were limited by their ability to articulate words physically. Access tutors and learning assistants were involved in every session and keen to take advantage of the opportunity to work on students' language skills in a new way. The work students produced in these groups and as individuals is proof that working with poetry is highly effective in developing and exercising language, thinking and creative skills – elements identified by educationists as critical to overall learning.

My sessions incorporated reading poetry, writing and reading back the work produced. We were based in the learning resource centre. It was more relaxed than a classroom, there were giant beanbags to sit on and we were surrounded by books. In the afternoons I worked on a play with performing arts students. I listened to research they produced, asked them about different ways of dramatising it and we brainstormed approaches – eg. would a poem work best in one scene and a short sketch in another? In these sessions, although students were not writing as much as in access sessions, they were articulating the creative approaches they wanted and the creative thinking that led to different scenes. It was a collaborative relationship.

We did not specify aims at the start, but there were concrete outcomes: a collection of work, a resource pack for tutors, video of the access students' performance, a play as well as poems and stories written by individual students. We also made a link with Arvon. Creative writers' own tools of the trade can have a profound impact on the acquisition of basic language skills as well as the development of more sophisticated language use. Poets in particular can offer approaches within the workshop format that improve self-expression and address fundamentals such as punctuation, syntax and editing in a creative way.

I created almost all the exercises I used during the residency because I was working with young people whose use of spoken and written language was so restricted. Exercises were based on poems or ideas in poems by a range of writers and many workshops began with questions because questions lead us to daydream and aspire to change.

What Schools Want

A school is a world in itself with rules, a hierarchy, sometimes a uniform and always its own values. A writer going into a school is often an outsider, unknown to most of the staff and students and sometimes a novelty or a treat. Writers are invited into schools in a number of ways, often through a third party organisation like the Poetry Society or a regional writers' agency. Sometimes the school approaches a writer directly and many writers build relationships with schools or particular teachers over the years, returning for special events like book or activities weeks. Over the 20+ years I worked in schools, I had a number of different briefs – day or half-day workshops, a full week, a residency lasting an academic year and another lasting two terms. Common to all of them has been communicating how I work as a writer and trying to show pupils, through practical writing exercises, how I go about creating poems and prose.

The attractions of working in a school are the creativity that exists among the young people gathered in a room to write and their enthusiasm for discovering new ways into writing or a new perspective. The demands of this kind of work are significant, though, and it is crucial to be well prepared, to think through what you want to do and why, and to have enough material to keep a workshop energetic and stimulating.

A school might want you to link your work specifically to the national curriculum or key stages. This is your choice. It might mean the difference between work or no work. But be careful – you write, you run workshops, but many writers are not qualified teachers. Your understanding of writing may be more instinctive than theoretical. Your workshop is an experience of writing – it will work because it's different to school. This is why residential workshops with schools in places like Arvon or Tŷ Newydd in Wales are so successful – they are a long way from the classroom. However, a good plan reassures a school that you have considered how the time will be spent.

I have worked with mixed ability groups and groups of gifted and talented pupils. In my experience, the main difference is the speed at which they work. One of the difficulties for a school in running writing workshops is that the normal classroom size is too big for an effective workshop. In practical terms, this raises the issue of teacher cover and who's available to support the writer. In some schools, I've run workshops alone with children, in others I've been supported by a teacher or teaching assistant.

To Do

- Make sure you have checked what public liability or other insurance you might need, and whether you need a Disclosure and Barring Service (DBS) check (you almost certainly will).
- Ask what arrangements the school has made for a teacher or assistant to be with you.
- Talk through your plan with a teacher if you have any concerns, check whether there are themes the class is currently looking at you might want to work with.
- Ask for a list of students taking part and stickers they can write their names on (but take your own stickers, just in case).
- Check whether any have special educational needs that you should be aware of.
- Ask the other adult in the workshop to participate in the writing exercises unless they're supporting a particular student.

Thirteen

Writing Exercises and Prompts

Writing is constant practice, like walking, playing an instrument, thinking. So every writer needs to keep challenging herself. I've collected some places to start – exercises tried and tested over years and adapted:

- Creative dialogue
- The creative power of form
- Is it you or are you making it up?
- Childhood
- Here and now in the material world
- Your people
- The news

Creative Dialogue

Whether you're starting to write or you've been doing it for a while, you are inevitably in dialogue with other writers in your head, as you read or listen. When you use this in your own writing, you'll find the creative impetus is powerful.

Writing Back

Find a poem you love and write your own version of it – this might mean modernising it, translating it into your own experience, answering it back. But keep its essence and pay tribute. Inua Ellams kept a diary of writing back after a residency in the National Poetry Library. It's fabulous. *Afterhours* (Nine Arches Press, 2017) contains the original poems and Ellams' own, as well as commentary on his process and finding the poems. Shazea Quraishi's poem series, *The Courtesan's Reply* is another example of writing back. It gives a voice to women who were silent when the work that inspired Quraishi, *The Caturbhani*, was written in 300 BC. Her series builds on that voice from the past. Read 'The Sixty-four Arts' for a great list poem that's also constructing a super-woman.

Praise Poems

The praise poem sits deep in oral culture globally. There are many examples in anthologies and online. I like the website africanpoems.net, founded by Martin White with poet Jack Mapanje as curatorial advisor. Read the Shumba Murambwi praise poem and write your own to a made-up creature or to another creature that means something to you.

A Song

Think about a song that matters to you. Write the title down, the singer or the band and the place you associate it with. Imagine yourself in one of the places where you've heard it. Are you singing along? Are you dancing? Who's with you and what line from the song jumps out? And find a surreal way of describing how the song makes you feel.

Memorial

Imagine one of the many memorials in old graveyards and

cemeteries is speaking to you. Write three questions you'd like to ask. Now write down the memorial's answers. Wander in an old cemetery before you start.

Look at Your House like Thomas Sheridan

Imagine lending your house to someone (why are you doing this?) Write a creative inventory of its contents. But read Thomas Sheridan's poem first:

A True and Faithful Inventory Of The Goods Belonging To Dr. Swift, Vicar of Laracor. Upon Lending His House To The Bishop of Meath, Until His Own Was Built
by Thomas Sheridan (1687–1738)

An Oaken, broken Elbow-Chair;
A Cawdle-Cup, without an Ear;
A battered, shattered Ash Bedstead;
A Box of Deal, without a Lid;
A Pair of Tongs, but out of Joint;
A Back-Sword Poker, without Point;
A Pot that's cracked across, around,
With an old knotted Garter bound;
An iron lock, without a Key;
A Wig, with hanging, grown quite grey;
A Curtain worn to Half a Stripe;
A Pair of Bellows, without Pipe;
A Dish, which might good Meat afford once;
An Ovid, and an old Corcordance;
A Bottle Bottom, Wooden Platter,
One is for Meal, and one for Water;
There likewise is a Copper Skillet,
Which runs as fast out as you fill it;

A Candlestick, Snuff dish, and Save-all,
And thus his Household Goods you have all.
These, to your Lordship, as a Friend,
Till you have built, I freely lend:
They'll save your Lordship for a Shift;
Why not, as well as Doctor Swift?

Cartoon Life

Venture into the worlds of Batman, Catwoman, Black Panther and the Incredible Hulk. Make up a new and diverse superhero for modern times. Put your new superhero in conversation with a traditional one. How do they get their powers? What is their biggest challenge?

Ekphrasis

There are countless examples of how writers use a work of art as the starting point for a poem. At its most basic, your writing begins when you look at the picture, sculpture, installation. Look first in silence without writing. Focus in – detail and close observation are the key as these examples show: 'Landscape with the Fall of Icarus' by William Carlos Williams is a deceptively simple poem describing the detail of a painting and recreating the same scene as the artist. 'Portraits of Tudor Statesmen' by the late U A Fanthorpe is a great poem to start writing about portraits. 'I would like to be a dot in a painting by Miro' by Moniza Alvi allows a writer to enter the art work imaginatively and write about the journey.

The Creative Power of Form

Some of us respond to a practical challenge, one that can keep our hands busy, so to speak, and free the images. The poet Marilyn Hacker puts it really well in an interview for the *Asheville Poetry*

Review in 2010 (Issue 19): '... for me at least working with a fixed form – whether it's a received form or one that I've made up – brings the unconscious into the work in a more active way. You have to be doing something other than thinking in a straightforward linear way, outside the story I want to tell, the mood I want to establish or the thing I want to describe. There is something that is nonlinear that has nothing to do with either narrative or emotion that is acting on the poem, an almost mathematical (or musical) requirement of syllables, stresses or sounds that have to be varied or repeated, a rhyme, sometimes all of these things together—these requirements can knock one's mind out of the box.' So with Hacker's words in your head ...

Rhyme, Rhythm, Syllables and Lines

There's no shortage of forms! Find a great guide to form and experiment. Or start with a simple rhyme scheme and stick to it but be inventive with those rhymes, break some rules, get lost in the challenge. If you've got plenty of energy, research a form you've never used before, inform yourself about its rules, see if you can do it, maybe with an unlikely subject. Look back to Patience Agbabi's poem in Part One to see an expert at work.

Harness the Dynamism of a Sequence

Build on the earlier ice-breaker challenge to make a list of titles for a sequence of poems. A sequence will inevitably draw you into thinking about form – do you make each poem the same shape and length? What forms might lend themselves to sequences?

Stuck? What's holding you back?

Read 'From the Frontier of Writing' by Seamus Heaney if you're at that point when you just can't. Visualise a physical frontier, describe it, and describe also what happens at the frontier post. Published in 1987 when there were checkpoints manned by the

British Army throughout Ireland, the poem is a brilliant example of visualisation (and more, obviously).

Sounds of Words

In Alastair Reid's poem 'Words' he instructs the reader what words to say in different situations, like 'Odd words (to be spoken out loud, for fun)'. The poem shows me the visceral impact of language, the impact on your body of verbs and nouns. The words you select for your own version of this might be a gift, or a toolkit for a particular situation. The sounds are as important as meaning.

Is It You or Are You Making It Up?

When you use the first person, the I, in a poem is it really you? Can I be someone else? Yes. Apart from the fact that we're all a mixture of many identities, it's handy to grasp quite early on in your writing life that you are allowed to make it up.

Witness

Put yourself in a photo as an observer. Write self-consciously about your role as an observer. Did you see something no-one else did? Did you miss the significance of an event?

Before and After

What has changed you? Write about yourself before and after...your birthday, a holiday, a haircut, redecorating, new glasses, moving the sofa. There is so much potential in even a minor change.

Your Fictional Visitors

Write five directions to your house warning your guest of something hidden, something difficult to see, what you see when you are almost there, where you have to double back, the door, what you can see in the window. An afterthought.

Ancestors

Like loads of people I've been transfixed by *Who Do You Think You Are*, celebrity family history. The great thing about ancestors is most of us can make the stories up. Read Vasko Popa's poem, 'In The Village of My Ancestors', with its intriguing character, George the Wolf. Write about going back to where your own ancestors lived (or might have).

The Animal Within

In Carl Sandburg's poem, 'Wilderness', he explores the idea of a menagerie inside the human narrator. What animals are within you? Where have they came from (and be imaginative here – they might have been an image on a fridge magnet) and what do they give you?

Obsession or Hobby?

Lists and obsessions are great for writing. Making a list is another a distraction, a move into fantasy or memory, depending on the subject. List the objects, tools, accoutrements of your obsession, or hobby, demands. Perhaps it's sewing, or football, fishing, playing guitar, baking, photography, collecting Bakelite. Most things that take up time have associated stuff – even trainspotting.

Childhood

Tap into memory. If you're hazy, look at old photos, think about the place or places where you lived, try and establish your earliest memory. I think of Dylan Thomas' poem, 'Fern Hill' and often re-read Majid Naficy's 'One Night I will Return to My Birthplace' in which, in exile, he describes the sky of his childhood. Here are some ideas to set you dreaming.

Childish Jobs

When you were a child, what jobs did you do at home? Sweeping, washing up, polishing shoes or the floor, going to the shop? Make some other tasks up. Who you were working alongside, or would have liked to work alongside?

Words of Childhood

Martina Evans writes about the word gazebo in a poem of the same name featured in Part One, exploring what she thought it meant when she was a child. Make a list of words you didn't understand when you were younger, but which fascinated you. Explore your confusion, the misunderstanding.

Animal Child

When you were a child what animal did you imagine yourself to be? Did you gallop around the playground, roar from under the table, stretch out your arms when it was windy? Believe you are an animal. Describe the sounds you make, the movements, what you smell and how you look. When you switch back to being human, describe that moment.

Teenage Places

When poet Lorna Thorpe writes about place this is often a way into an emotional or psychological state. Read her poem 'Lower Market Street, 1973' in *A Ghost in My House* (Arc Publications, 2008) and remember a moment in adolescence, approaching adulthood. It's a time when we're intensely aware of place, when streets, nightclubs, shops, parks, views and our routes to and from home, school or college, are imprinted for life. So a place name with a date is a starting point for writing about youth.

Meeting Yourself

Grace Nichols writes about the 'ghost / of my childhood' in her poem 'If I were to Meet'. She describes 'a brown girl gazing at fish shapes' as if the girl is a stranger. And, of course, our childhood selves are strangers. You can use this idea and choose to meet yourself at any point in your life (or at many) and give yourself a way of exploring personal themes from a different perspective.

Here and Now in the Material World

Sometimes I want to read a poem that is as simple as a moment. And so sometimes I want my writing to be as connected as possible to the stuff that we live among. Joy Harjo's poem 'Praise the Rain' is an example of how to think yourself into the here and now. Then again, so's a YouTube tutorial when you need to fix something.

The Street

What's happening out on your street? Do you eavesdrop on people talking, can you catch some conversation? Is someone singing with headphones in, or a car driver beeping their horn? Is there an ambulance outside someone's house, or a child having a tantrum? It might be as small as someone dropping a can. It might be as big a thing as a massive lorry trying to squeeze through a narrow road. Describe yourself watching. Imagine saying something out loud to yourself.

Walking

If I have a problem it can often be solved by walking. Take something that is troubling you out of the house or visualise a walk you're familiar with. Identify places on that walk that can give you a new perspective, calm you down. What happens to the problem when you walk? What landmarks, plants, sights console you?

YouTube

Watch a YouTube video with instructions. Include a phrase you found useful.

Drought

Think of days of heat. Find Robin Gow's poem, 'rice & rain' at The Poetry Foundation online and Chris Magadza's poem 'The Breaking of The Drought' on Poetry International. In parts of the world drought lasts months or years. Now start writing. How does it feel when drought breaks and rain falls? Can you smell rain coming? Describe what the sky looks like, the change in the light. How does your body react to drought ending. What does your skin notice? Describe where the rain gathers, gaps in the storm, how animals and birds react.

Your Old Addresses

Make a list of everywhere you've ever lived, including short stays, though not holidays. If you don't remember the address, note the town or city and area. When you've finished, chose one place and list at least five people you associate with it. You don't need to know their names, a brief description will do. Chose one of those five and write about them or in their voice.

Your People

The poet Ann Sansom has a beautiful poem called 'What friends are for'. Whenever I read it I can picture myself somewhere with the people I've relied on for company, advice, laughs, and who'll listen. The people around us, friends and family, shape us so they'll shape our poems too.

The Match

Remember a sports fixture, match or a game, and recreate it as you write. When was it? Where did it take place? What are the sounds of this sport? Name a couple of players. Who were you with? There might have been an interruption – what was it?

Visiting Someone You Love

How do you travel to visit the person you love and how are your journeys different? There's something they don't know about you. What is it?

Old Jobs, New Jobs

How many jobs have you had? Start with some notes about your work history, paid or unpaid. Include casual work, jobs you had as a teenager, maybe delivering newspapers or babysitting, volunteer work. Settle on one of those jobs, describe where you worked, someone you worked for or with and something they said to you.

Lovers and Classic Cars

Catherine Smith writes about a boyfriend's car in her poem 'Zephyr', a memory prompted by her sensible Passat. She uses the car to express the urgency of sex at 17, and freedom. The car is described as vividly as the lives of young lovers and the period – 1979. The poem uses it as a self-contained world.

Read the poem, list cars from childhood and adolescence. It's important to have the make, colour, date Write using Smith's premise – where would you expect to see it?

Zephyr
by Catherine Smith

As I return to my sensible Passat
in Tesco's car park, I still
expect to see the Zephyr, brooding –
that fuck-off hulk of a motor
you bought for three hundred quid
from a Birmingham art student, 1979;
two tons of scratched black metal,
lacquered red and orange flames
licking the doors and fenders.
I remember the M1 muffled with
blinding snow, Led Zeppelin, full blast;
fingers freezing inside my gloves,
lighting your Marlboroughs,
handing them over as you squinted
into the low sun. I loved your dark hair
curling into the nape of your neck,
your white, even teeth. And always,
always, your hand pressed on my knee
would dry my mouth, part my legs –
you'd find a slip-road, park in a clearing
and unravel me from my layers,
thumbing my jeans to my knees.
You kept your scratchy sweater on,
the one that flamed my nipples.
The leatherette bench seat where we slid
 – our breath, fogging the blue air, while
the engine tutted and you – you,
pressing me down, exploding
inside me like a meteor shower.
Ah, the sex, the raw, tricky sex

we had in that car – I remember too
the times it flounced to a standstill
or refused to start after a bellyful of fuel –
you'd sit tight, I'd be sent to recruit
nonplussed lorry drivers to help push
the bastard off forecourts.
That night in hushed Moseley where
it sputtered messily up a side-street,
coughed and died, on our way to a party –
and I'm wide-eyed, Southern-posh,
can in hand, Could we have
some water, please, for the car,

yes, sorry, we're students, sorry
from a startled, aproned woman
halfway through peeling spuds.
And if I saw it now, would I have the guts
to snap the locks, hot-wire it,
listen to the engine gurgle, ease
its bulk towards the exit, my foot
fluttering the brake as your fingers
once fluttered inside me? Rummage
through the glove compartment
for your stash of Wrigley's Freshmint,
or one final, desiccated cigarette,
mutter, Come on, you useless pile of crap,
you freak, you ghost – seventeen again,
rotten with desire – would I laugh
as the beast jerked into life, could I
grip the wheel, peer into low sun,
jam my foot down, and head north?

from *Otherwhere* (Smith|Doorstop, 2012)

The News

If you have to write a poem in response to an incident in the news, you might want to sit on it for a while, especially if it's written after watching rather than participating, especially if it's written about people a long way away. I have many brilliant poems and collections on my bookshelves that engage with the modern world politically – Chris Abani's *Kalakuta Republic* is one, Grace Nichols' *The Fat Black Woman's Poems* is another. I think of Adrienne Rich's poem, 'Diving into the wreck' and the lines, 'I came to see the damage that was done / and the treasures that prevail.' There are many brilliant political poets globally who have been writing for years. We can all learn from them.

What can a dinner party show us about a century's leaders?

Fadhil Al Azzawi's poem, 'Feast in Candlelight' imagines 'the 20th century in its long-dim hall.' Who would you sit at the 20th century's table – or any other century you choose, past or future? What is being served. What is happening outside?

City Transformed

Urban farmers are turning disused or neglected land into vegetable patches. Write a manifesto for your village, town or city. Start with the phrase: I will plant. You can plant mango trees next to pear trees, a rainforest next to a shopping centre, mix up the real with the impossible to plant freedom, a new language. Keep repeating that phrase, I will plant.

The Unsaid and Unwritten

When I read 'Glory Be to the Gang Gang Gang' by Momtaza Mehri it was the first time I'd seen Filet-O-Fish in a poem. I was reminded of Frank O'Hara and every poet who dares to write beyond what's expected of them. You can find Mehri's poem on the Academy of American Poets website. Make a list of what's not "suitable" for a poem and write those poems.

Manifesto

When I came across Roger Robinson's manifesto 'Success is on You', I was knocked out. So while this exercise won't necessarily end up as a poem, it will help you focus on what you want. His manifesto was first published as tweets and then collected in the UK magazine, *Poetry Review*, autumn 2017. I related to so much of it. But your task is a little different. Go through your writing and identify your themes. Is there a place you go back to? An idea? A specific image or person? Certain colours, or animals? Write a 10-point manifesto that outlines your intentions. How will your writing change you? How will it change the world? The statements you write will come from questions you ask yourself about your creative life. Some art manifestos have defined a movement, some have been recited in public, some have set out how the artists intend to live and work. What impact will your writing have?

Fourteen
Identity, Words in Gardens and Questions

We all work in different ways, but there will come a time when you'll want to dig deep into a way of working, a way of writing, or a subject with all its facets and different pathways. It's fascinating to read work by poets whose collections go back to a central idea, a guiding principal or thought. It's not essential for any of us – the accumulation of poems is sometimes slow, like strata and the way they're connected won't be quite as obvious.

I've chosen three areas that I've become interested in as I've researched poem models for workshops. Here I describe more detailed, step-by-step approaches:

- Identity – working with a theme from several angles
- Words – the perspective of visual artists
- Asking questions – Pablo Neruda's final collection

Identity – are you a shapeshifter, a boaster and who do you eat with?

The Furniture Game

I first discovered the furniture game in Sandy Brownjohn's *Does it Have to Rhyme?* and many writers use it. It's a good warm up exercise, the formula's even spread into advertising copy. It's a staple because it gets results so quickly, like shaking the tension out of your shoulders before singing. Since coming across it, I've found many examples where this phrase 'I am' is a framework for a poem. The furniture game is an exercise in metaphor. It shows the power of metaphor against simile. As a workshop leader you need this exercise to be quick and simple.

Your instructions can be basic – describe yourself as different objects. That's why it's called the furniture game. Give an example that shows contrasting descriptions of the same thing, say a sofa … are you Dali's red lips sofa in his museum in Spain? Are you an old studded leather Chesterfield in an antique shop? Are you a stained and ripped old sofa bed at the tip? Each line starts with 'I am' and is a detailed description of an object or place. There's no right or wrong answer. Here are some I use:

- an item of furniture
- an item of clothing
- shoes
- a time of day (be precise)
- a street
- an aspect of the weather (e.g. hurricane, mist)
- a public building (anywhere in the world – name it)
- an ordinary building (anywhere in the world)
- a sound

Sound is a good one to end on. I don't use animals because there's another exercise you can use on 'the animal within'. Move on quickly and don't give people time to worry or think too hard. It works best with fast responses. At the end I ask people to give it a title and read aloud one by one without explanation or apology. The furniture game has a 3,000-year history. Its basic premise – shape shifting – is evident throughout literature.

Taliesin the Shapeshifter

When I started to look for poems that seemed to work in the same way as the furniture game I felt I was picking up a thread. I remembered Charles Causley's poem 'I Am the Song'. But then I discovered a poem translated by Welsh scholar, Sir Ifor Williams, 'I am Taliesin, I sing perfect metre'. Poems in the manuscript it comes from, *The Book of Taliesin*, have been dated from the 12th and 13th centuries and were the work of various poets but there's an argument some are older. Taliesin himself was a poet from the 6th century. The short translation by Williams I use is a taste of another world of thought. I guide people through its structure, asking them to write their own lines to replace Williams'. The structure of the poem is robust. Unlike the furniture game, it's a poem to do at the end of a day or in the middle of a week, when peoples' writing is starting to move up a notch. It goes to the heart of identity and allows people of all ages to respond at their own level – children of eight years old up to adults. You'll need to read Ifor Williams' translation for the instructions below to make sense.

I start by reading the poem and explain we're doing our own version of it. I explain why some of the claims were unusual at the time: undersea exploration was unknown at the time, people may have observed echoes, but did not give scientific explanations for them. As boasts go, here are some big ones. I don't go into a lot of history but I explain Taliesin was a poet and hero.

- To write your own version, start with a boast – and write it with your name i.e. I am Jackie, I make the best pizza. The more outrageous, the better, but they can be as simple as: I'm a good friend, always there for you.

- Think of a question you've always wanted to know the answer to, but don't. Start the body of the poem with it: I know why the sky is blue. This is your second line.

- Next, write down a list of observations about the world (three or four) starting with 'why?' to follow on from the first line ... For example: why my cat sleeps all day, why plastic floats, why the smell of petrol makes me sick.

- If there's enough time you can continue adding to this list, as in the original. Otherwise, skip on.

- Now think of something that changes regularly. The beginning of the next line will change to: I know where ... mirroring a line in the poem about the cuckoos of summer. It could be something cyclical, or just observational. People have come up with amazing examples like: I know where my pain goes when I am comfortable, I know where my tears go when I am happy, I know where my thoughts go when I forget them.

- Onto exploration and the line about the beasts at the bottom of the sea. Think of unexplored places like the Milky Way, the brain, Mars and imagine what or who lives there (aliens are banned). You start this line with: I know what (or who) ...

- Onto things that can't be counted, as in the spears in battle and drops in a shower. Hairs on the head, stones on a beach, cells in a drop of blood, bacteria on a sponge ... This list can be fun, so extend it or chose two of your best ideas. These lines start: How many ...

- This section ends with knowledge of historical events as in the poem. The line starts with: I know why ... This can tie in with topical events (I say history starts a second ago) or older events like: I know why Henry killed his wives.

- At times, I make the end of the workshop poem simpler than the original, leaving out the Taliesin story, although if there's time, it's a challenge to summarise a life as the original does.

- Finally, imagine you have changed shape between animals and objects. In the poem animals and objects are carefully chosen: salmon to show wisdom, dog for loyalty, the axe usefulness or strength etc. So your choices influence the story you want to tell about yourself.
- End by repeating your first line – your name and the boast.

These poems read in a group gain fantastic momentum and are often moving. A new version of *The Book of Taliesin*, translated by Gwyneth Lewis and Rowan Williams was published in 2020.

'The Song of Amheirgin'

'The Song of Amheirgin' was written more than 3,000 years ago in Ireland. Robert Graves wrote the version I use. This poem reads to me like a call and response with its neat symmetry on the page and in the lines. What makes it even more interesting is the two questions embedded at the end of the first two stanzas. The structure, like the furniture game, is easy to follow although I guide writers through by identifying specific categories line by line. The first stanza contains three lines about the weather, two about animals, an injury and two marvels. It is important to be specific about place; the descriptions work by shifting focus from the detail to landscape. Questions make time for reflection – both stem from archetypes, both are observations made interesting by the phrase 'who but I'. The second and third stanzas are lists of much more powerful images, becoming increasingly dangerous towards the end. Read aloud, versions of this poem are like incantations.

'They Tell Me I am Lost'

The poem by Maurice Kenny, 'They Tell Me I am Lost' offers another dimension to 'I am' with the roll call of physical attributes in the first stanza. The second stanza's introduction of a personal chant is sustained through much of the poem into places of refuge before ending with the more familiar list of animal and object identities. So an exercise can be relatively short or much longer, depending on time. The categories are straightforward, but as always, the best versions bring in something new like urban imagery. It is long but it's important to read it fully – the poem builds in resonance by stacking up images. The first stanza and second stanzas could be an exercise in themselves because the ideas are so interesting and accessible. The third and fifth lines: 'my thought …' and 'my spirit eats with …' produce fascinating and thoughtful results, as indeed does Kenny's final line, 'I am the string, the bow and the arrow'.

I stress the importance of this line as a sign off and a summary of an individual's power. Kenny is going further than a simple 'I am' here and suggesting the narrator has the force of a trinity: three component parts needed to work. So this part of the exercise demands that the writer thinks about an object as well as its components. It could translate as: 'I am the table, the feast and the tree'. It's infinitely flexible and offers enormous potential for self-expression.

Words – the perspective of visual artists

Almost every time I've used the work of visual artists I've been working with groups of children or adults outside in the countryside and city. Hamish Fulton and Richard Long's texts focus on pattern, detail and landmarks through looking and concentrating on the physical world. I turned to Fulton when I was challenged to come up with a project for a small rural primary school, working with young children, focused on exploring and expressing their thoughts about their environment. Fulton's walking poems provided a structure I could explain easily and adapt, a methodology for looking and noting that was close to the experience of forming a poem. Fulton's careful observations offered a way to slow down and savour the marvels of pond dipping. In 'Song Path' he notes the number of paces he takes and what is happening in the sky and earth. In 'Seven Days Walking and Seven Nights Camping in a Wood Scotland March 1985', everything he observes is listed in capital letters, as a block of text, each phrase and word divided by a stop. His observations include brown pine needles, a few flakes of falling snow, sound of the small stream. Fulton regards walking itself as an art form and his approach enables a writer to concentrate on the smallest detail and allow that detail to speak. It is an expression of our oldest activity as people. I think of the Wordworths walking 20 miles a day, I think of great movements of people since the beginning of human history – for discovery, by force or in desperation. Baudelaire was a flaneur of city streets and Brazilian artist Paulo Nazareth is one of many continuing the walking tradition with his 'Africa Notebooks', recording slave routes from Johannesburg to Lyon.

Word Walk in the Style of Hamish Fulton

Wander through a park, beach, city or wood. Start by counting out the number of steps you take. Stop. Instruct workshop participants (or yourself) to look right, left, up or down. Note all you see (touch, hear, smell) as you are doing this, but sparingly. Focus on physical detail. Move on, count more steps and change where you look. Look down, too. Study examples of how Fulton does it – the shape on the page is important. This is a poem in which appearance matters as much as the words' individual meanings.

Words in an Orchard

Another artist who interested me was Richard Long. I first saw an exhibition of his work in London at the end of the 20th century and was struck by how he put text on gallery walls. One work, for example, is a single line:

A day's walk across Dartmoor following the drift of the clouds.

When words are on gallery walls each letter has to earn its right to be present. The spareness of these text works, and the reader's knowledge of the experience they are based on are what helped in a project in an orchard. I was working with a group of people with learning disabilities and their teacher suggested we needed to take a more visual approach to words. I thought too about Jenny Holzer's placing of single words and phrases in the landscape. So I borrowed the visual artist's boldness to intervene in the tamed world of an RHS garden, ordered to within an inch of its life, contained in neat ponds, paths and beds. An artist friend gave me materials. An apple orchard provided names, including my favourite, The Bloody Ploughman, written in colour and capitals and placed on a board at the foot of the trunk. We all loved that one and the meaning of the words stretched far beyond the name of the apple, to the history of agricultural labourers and poverty. And with new understanding of how landscape and language intersect we moved onto writing a Circle of Words, based on Long's statement,

> I can make a circle of words, I can make a circle of stones, I can make a circle of mud with my hands on a wall, I can walk in a circle for one hundred miles. It is a completely adaptable image and form and system.

Richard Long, 1988

Language of Flowers

In Ian Hamilton Finlay's garden, Little Sparta, he carved nine stones and arranged them in a circle like a clock face. The inscriptions include: FURY EX-LARKSPUR and RESTLESS EX-PERIWINKLE. They come from 'Ovidian Flowers', a nine-line poem from his collection *Blue Sail* (2002) in which he changes the common name of nine flowers into an adjective or noun describing an emotion or human quality, so for example one line reads, 'Hearts-ease became Courage'.

When I was preparing to work in the garden of an old country house with Capability Brown-designed grounds I needed starting points for poems with people who had special educational needs. Glass houses had been used to grow orchids for a mega-rich owner, and the parkland around the house was punctuated by magnificent oaks. I was put in a so-called Japanese garden with a pond and small arched bridge. I wanted to avoid the obvious but somehow refer to the idea of a deliberately created environment. The poem was an easy model to explain, repetitive and fun, a collecting poem which I could use as the basis of two lists in which words were almost paired randomly. As it turned out, the pairing was conscious. Support workers enjoyed the challenge of finding flower names among the rocks and discussing what emotions or qualities particular plants suggested, based on shapes or colours, using that wonderfully obliging and transformative bridge, 'became'. Our versions of 'Ovidian Flowers', whatever Hamilton Finlay's intentions were, became games which opened up the process of writing. It was a funny little place that bore no resemblance to a true Japanese garden, a place created for the imagination of an old colonialist, but which nevertheless became a shady place where foxgloves thrived and we clambered over rocks, managing not to fall into the pond.

Asking Questions – Pablo Neruda's final collection

We learn by asking questions. Often random, unanswerable, they confront taboos, they make us squirm and laugh. We ask them at difficult moments and how we respond can define a relationship with a child or a lover. Questions are common to all of us: plumbers, farmers, child-minders, mechanics, dressmakers, scientists, inventors, marketers, nurses. How do I mend that? Why's it broken? How do I make yellow? Why do men buy beer with nappies? Without questions, there's no thought, society, language.

In *The Book of Questions* Neruda reaches to the essence of poetry and metaphor. He could have written these poems as statements. They would have been one man's view of the world. But as questions, he allows us to experience the journey he is on as he searches for a way of expressing himself. Some may seem simple, but most have no literal or single answers. They demand an equally engaged and creative response. To read and consider them, we must be open. We must visualise and from there, stretch into the metaphysical.

To appreciate the force of these questions, you must have the book. The translation I use is by William O'Daly. There are 320 questions grouped into 74 poems reminiscent of koans, the meditative Zen practice. They were the last poems Neruda wrote before he died: the summing up of a life of writing.

Using Neruda's Questions in Workshops

I read examples aloud, quickly, selectively and ask people to write questions of their own in Neruda's style. I emphasise the visual and physical world – objects, colours, places, and the environment. I repeat two or three of Neruda's, explaining how he focuses on colour with rubies and pomegranates, for example, and ask why it's more interesting to make that comparison as a question than a statement. I ask for at least 10 questions because the more you write the more interesting the questions become. Some can be linked, but they don't have to be. As you write, you find a momentum and the bizarre, the surreal emerges. Neruda's questions provoke thought, often a complex emotional response and most have no answers.

Questions in Clay

When I worked alongside ceramicist Julian Belmonte to run workshops for ninety 10- and 11-year-olds at a Surrey school we needed an efficient way of combining clay and words. The workshops also had to draw on children's experiences visiting a restored air raid shelter nearby. It was autumn, a time of year that crops up in many of Neruda's questions. We couldn't use many words because Julian had to press them into clay discs. To start with we talked a lot and I asked the children to call questions out, then to write a list, to think about sitting in the dark in the shelter with bombers flying overhead. I handed out strips of paper and asked them to write out their two most surprising questions, one on each side.

Afterword

Work hard and be nice to people is an aphorism my daughter showed me in an art publication just after she graduated. It was made into a poster by Anthony Burrill in 2004 who attributed the line to an overheard conversation in a supermarket about what makes a happy life.

It's subversive in its simplicity and appeals to me for that reason. A poem has the same sense of being complete, of preserving a moment when you eavesdropped and were grabbed.

I don't question why I write, sew, grow vegetables, walk, or cook. Writing is a necessary part of my life, even when I'm not writing, and that's quite often. It used to be a physical need – if I didn't write I was very hard to live with. Now it's a controlled pleasure, a place for connections I can't make anywhere else. But it's become a lot harder to keep going because of distractions that sometimes feel like deliberate attempts to de-rail writers and artists. I mean capitalism's great invention, the winner.

Over the years I've begun to understand why I've had long periods not writing. An artist friend has suggested there's a seasonal pattern – I write less in summer when I'm busy on the allotment. I think there's more. No-poem zones take me away from the success/failure deception. The earth and sewing machine return belief in the moment, in dead-heading, mending, cutting a pattern, concentration. They are places I train myself to keep away from the noise.

But I do it in the hope that when I'm pulling the curtains back to see what the weather's doing, that today's the day to get back to writing, it's there, jostling to be said. During my first few days away after lockdown I didn't touch my notebook, I was too busy enjoying myself in my daughter's chosen city, but on the Eurostar coming home I wrote four poems.

Not writing helps me listen, too, reminds me to read, to take enjoyment from a perfect chocolate brownie. And when I am ready to write again, I think those lines are more grounded, like the row of chard seeds, like the stitches of a hem.

And what luck, to be among people who write, paint, make music, take photographs, because they have to be true to themselves, generous people who translate, edit magazines, put on events, share insecurities, celebrate small rewards, offer solutions to failure, dry spells and suggest ways of keeping going as we nudge craft and convention to their limits in a series of small acts of resistance.

Endnotes

1. Ruth Padel, The Sunday Poem, No 26, *The Independent,* 5 June 1999
2. Adrienne Rich: https://www.poetryfoundation.org/poets/eleanor-ross-taylor
3. Wright, George T.: 'Hendiadys and Hamlet'. *PMLA*, vol. 96, no. 2, 1981, pp. 168–193. JSTOR, www.jstor.org/stable/461987. Accessed 5 Sept. 2021.
4. Lavinia Greenlaw: 'Sylvia Plath, Reflections on Her Legacy', the *Guardian* 8.2.2013
5. Olive Senior: Writers Trust of Canada Margaret Lawrence Lecture Series 2019
6. Kim Moore: *The Poetry Paper*, Issue 10, 2013
7. Bernadine Evaristo: The *Guardian,* 19 Oct 2019
8. Susan Sontag, *At the Same Time* (Penguin, 2013)
9. Vicki Feaver: 'Presiding Spirits: Vicki Feaver talks to Judy Brown' (*Magma* 54)
10. Mimi Khalvati: 'Child: A Recommendation by Marilyn Hacker' (Carcanet Blog 11. p. 38 January 25 2012)
11. Wallace Stevens, from *Men Made out of Words* by Wallace Stevens, 1947
12. Bertolt Brecht, trans. David Constantine and Tom Khun
13. *Poetry Review,* guest eds Moniza Alvi and Esther Morgan, Spring 2013
14. 'The Wife of Bafa' by Patience Agbabi from *Telling Tales* (Canongate, 2015)
15. Erykah Badu: https://i-d.vice.com/en_uk/article/xwxkxj/erykah-badu-on-riccardo-tisci-and-channeling-grace-jones
16. Emily Dickinson from Emily Dickinson Museum online. Quote sourced from L342a, 1870: *The Letters of Emily Dickinson*, eds Thomas H. Johnson and Theodora Ward (Cambridge, Mass.: The Belknap Press of Harvard University Press, 1958).
17. Statement from UNESCO on World Poetry Day, March 21
18. Warsan Shire's profile on Poetry Foundation website.
19. Audre Lorde from *Sister Outsider* (Crossing Press Berkeley, 2007). 'Poetry Is Not a Luxury' was first published in 1977 in *Chrysalis: A Magazine of Female Culture.*

20 Jenny Holzer's website: https://projects.jennyholzer.com/

21 Audre Lorde from 'Poetry is not a luxury' in *Sister Outsider* (The Crossing Press, 1984)

22 Marilyn Hacker interview on translation for *Book Culture* November 2016, https://www.bookculture.com/blog/2016/10/27/qa-marilyn-hacker-translation

23 *An ABC of Translating Poetry* by Willis Barnstone at poets.org

24 Tara Bergin from 'Pronounced Chockitch', *MPT* No.3 2018

25 *Poetry Translation for Newcomers* by Jamie Lee Searle, researched and produced for The Stephen Spender Trust, https://www.stephen-spender.org/wp-content/uploads/2021/04/Poetry-Translation-for-Newcomers_SST-Resource.pdf

26 Sasha Dugdale in *MPT* No. 3 2017

27 'In Conversation with Susan Wicks & Valérie Rouzeau', Arc Publications 2014

28 *MPT* No. 2, 2020

29 Eleanor Goodman, 'Interview with Shanghai Literary Review', June 10, 2019 https://www.shanghailiterary.com/tslr-online/2019/4/17/eleanor-goodman-interview

30 Ted Hughes, 'The Art of Poetry', *The Paris Review* No. 71

Quoted and Referenced Poems

Chapter 1

'The Flea' by John Donne (first published 1633)
'Daddy' and 'Edge' by Sylvia Plath from *Ariel* (Faber, 1965)
'Thoughts After Ruskin' by Elma Mitchell from *People Etcetera: New and Selected Poems* (Peterloo Poets, 1987)
'Lapwings' by Alison Brackenbury from *Then* (Carcanet, 2013)
'Woman as Artist' by Eleanor Ross Taylor from *Captive Voices: New and Selected Poems 1960–2008* (Louisiana State Press, 2009)
'Warming her pearls' by Carol Ann Duffy from *Selling Manhattan* (Anvil, 1987)
'Money Talks' by Carol Ann Duffy from *Selling Manhattan* (Anvil, 1987)

Chapter 2

'Being Fifty' by Selima Hill from *Violet* (Bloodaxe Books, 1997)
'Song of Solomon' by Liz Lochhead from *Dreaming Frankenstein and collected poems 1967–1984* (Polygon, 1984)
'The Song of Songs', the Bible
'The Fat Black Woman Goes Shopping' by Grace Nichols from *The Fat Black Woman's Poems* (Virago, 1984)
'Brief Lives' by Olive Senior from *Gardening in the Tropics* (Insomniac Press, 2005)
'Yet Another Poem of Struggle' by Meiling Jin from *Gifts from My Grandmother* (Sheba, 1985)

Chapter 3

'The Ice-Cream Man' and 'The Butchers' by Michael Longley from *Gorse Fires* (Jonathan Cape, 1991)
'Miss Snooks Poetess' by Stevie Smith from *Collected Poems and Drawings of Stevie Smith* (Faber, 2015)
'Forgetfulness' by Vicki Feaver from *Second Wind* (Saltire Society, 2015)
'The Language of the Brag' by Sharon Olds from *The Matter of this World New and Selected Poems* (Slow Dancer, 1987)
'More fun than Nigella' by Lorna Thorpe from *Sweet Torture of Breathing* (Arc Publications, 2011)
'The Language of the Brag' by Sharon Olds from *Satan Says* (University of Pittsburgh Press, 1980)
'Ghazal (after Hafez)' by Mimi Khalvati from *The Meanest Flower* (Carcanet, 2007)
'You', 'Royal Society for the Promotion of Loneliness', 'Happiness returns,

after a long absence', by Penelope Shuttle from *Sandgrain and Hourglass* (Bloodaxe Books, 2010)

'The Sari' by Moniza Alvi from *Split World: Poems 1990-2005* (Tarset: Bloodaxe Books, 2008)

'11 The Camp' by Moniza Alvi from *At the Time of Partition* (Bloodaxe Books, 2013)

Chapter 4

'Digging' by Edward Thomas from *Last Poems* (Selwyn & Blount, 1918)

'Zaatar' by Sarah Maguire from *Almost the Equinox: Selected Poems* (Chatto & Windus, 2015)

'The Doll's House' by Patience Agbabi from *Poetry Review* (2013)

'Pepys and a nightingale' by Janet Sutherland from *Home Farm* (Shearsman Books, 2019)

'Ode to a Nightingale' by John Keats (first published 1819)

Chapter 5

'Hiss' by Jay Bernard from *Surge* (Chatto & Windus, 2019)

'The Fitting' by Edna St Vincent Millay from *Poetry Magazine* (October 1938)

'The Fall' by Pauline Stainer from *Parable Island* (Bloodaxe Books, 1999)

'The Bean Eaters' by Gwendolyn Brooks from *Selected Poems* (Harper & Row, 1963)

'How To Behave With The Ill' by Julia Darling from *Indelible, Miraculous: The Collected Poems of Julia Darling* (Arc Publications, 2015)

'The Negro Speaks of Rivers' by Langston Hughes from *The Collected Poems of Langston Hughes* (Random House, 1995)

'Gazebo' by Martina Evans from *Burnfort, Las Vegas* (Anvil Press Poetry, 2014)

'Architecture' by Chase Twitchell from *The Snow Watcher* (Bloodaxe Books, 1999)

'Lunch' and 'Exodus' by Lotte Kramer from *More New & Selected Poems* (Rockingham Press, 2015)

Chapter 6

'The Joy of Writing' by Wisława Szymborska from *View with a grain of sand: selected poems,* trans. S. Baranczak & C. Cavanagh (Faber, 1995)

'Variations On The Word Love' by Margaret Atwood from *True Stories* (Simon and Schuster, 1981)

'Sonnets from the Portugese 43' Elizabeth Barrett Browning (first published 1850)

'Resignation' by Nikki Giovanni from *The Collected Poetry of Nikki Giovanni:*

1968–1998 (Harper Perennial Modern Classics, 2007)
'Homage to my Hips' by Lucille Clifton from *Two-Headed Woman* (University of Massachusetts Press, 1980)
'Still I Rise' by Maya Angelou from *And Still I Rise* (Random House, 1978)
'The Hill We Climb' by Amanda Gorman from *The Hill We Climb: an inauguration poem* (Penguin, 2021)
'Home' by Warsan Shire from https://www.facinghistory.org/standing-up-hatred-intolerance/warsan-shire-home
'The Colonel' by Carolyn Forché from *The Country Between Us* (HarperCollins, 1981)
'Crossing Back' by Choman Hardi from *Considering the Women* (Bloodaxe Books, 2015)
'On the 70th Anniversary of the Warsaw Uprising' by Maria Jastrzębska from *Small Odysseys* (Waterloo Press, 2021)
'Poem (I lived in the first century of world wars)' by Muriel Rukeyser, from *Princess, Priestess, Poet: The Sumerian Temple Hymns of Enheduanna* by Betty De Shong Meador (University of Texas Press, 2009)

Chapter 7

'A Bengali Woman in Britain' by Safuran Ara (trans. Debjani Chatterjee from *Songs in Exile/Probashir Pala: A bilingual collection* (Sheffield Libraries, 1999)
'At the Edge of a Field, a Pair of Shoes' by Wang Xiaoni (trans. Gordon T Osing and De-An Wu Swihart from *At the Edge of a Field, a Pair of Shoes* (Salt Hill, 1998)

Chapter 11

'This is a photograph of me' by Margaret Atwood from *The Circle Game* (House of Anansi Press, 1998)
'The Idea of Ancestry' by Etheridge Knight from *The Essential Etheridge Knight* (University of Pittsburgh Press, 1986)
'They tell me I am lost' by Maurice Kenny from *Harper's Anthology of Twentieth Century Native American Poetry* (HarperCollins, 1988)
'Song of Myself' by Walt Whitman from *Leaves of Grass* (1855)
'Dogwoman' by Deryn Rees-Jones from *Burying the Wren* (Seren, 2012)
'The quartz pebble' by Vasko Popa from *Selected Poems* (Penguin, 1969)
'Soap Suds' by Louis MacNeice from *Collected Poems* (Faber, 2007)
'The Book of Blood' by Vicki Feaver from *The Book of Blood* (Jonathan Cape, 2006)
'Inventing' by Penelope Shuttle from *Redgrove's Wife* (Bloodaxe Books, 2006)
'Being a Grandmother' and 'Portrait of my lover as a spoon' by Selima Hill from *Gloria: Selected Poems* (Bloodaxe Books, 2008)

Chapter 12

'Lineage' by Ted Hughes from *Crow: From the Life and the Songs of the Crow* (Faber, 1970)
'The Bridge of Toys' by Carol Ann Duffy from *Meeting Midnight* (Faber, 1999)
'Cows' by Ted Hughes from *Collected Poems* (Faber, 2003)
'The Sound Collector' by Roger McGough from *All the Best – The Selected Poems of Roger McGough* (Puffin, 2004)
'The Guardians' by George Mackay Brown from *The Collected Poems of George Mackay Brown* (John Murray, 2006)
'Fairy Tale' by Miroslav Holub, translated from the Czech by George Theiner, from *The Rattle Bag*, eds Seamus Heaney and Ted Hughes (Faber, 1972)
'I am Taliesin' translated by Sir Ifor Williams from *The School Bag* eds Seamus Heaney and Ted Hughes (Faber, 1997)
'Words' by Alastair Reid from *Ounce, Dice, Trice* (NYRB Children's Collection, 2009)
'Morning' by Dionne Brand from *Can I buy a slice of sky?: poems from Black, Asian and American Indian cultures* ed Grace Nichols (Blackie, 1991)
'Wilderness' by Carl Sandburg from *The Complete Poems of Carl Sandburg* (Harcourt Brace Iovanovich, 1970)

Chapter 13

'The Sixty-four Arts' by Shazea Quraishi from *Quraishi, Shazea, The Courtesan's Reply* (Flipped Eye Publishing, 2012)
'A True and Faithful Inventory Of The Goods Belonging To Dr. Swift, Vicar of Laracor. Upon Lending His House To The Bishop of Meath, Until His Own Was Built' by Thomas Sheridan from *The Poems of Thomas Sheridan* (University of Delaware Press,1994)
'Landscape with the Fall of Icarus' by William Carlos Williams from *Pictures from Breughel and other poems* (New Directions, 1967)
'Portraits of Tudor Statesmen' by UA Fanthorpe from *Selected Poems* (Peterloo Poets, 1986)
'I would like to be a dot in a painting by Miro' by Moniza Alvi from *Split World: Poems 1990–2005* (Bloodaxe Books, 2008)
'From the Frontier of Writing' by Seamus Heaney from *Haw Lantern* (Faber, 1987)
'In The Village of My Ancestors' by Vasko Popa from *Selected Poems* (Penguin, 1969)
'The Quartz Pebble' by Vasko Popa translated by Anne Pennington from *Complete Poems 1953-87* (Anvil Press Poetry, 2011)
'Wilderness' by Carl Sandburg from *The Complete Poems of Carl Sandburg* (Harcourt Brace Iovanovich, 1970)
'Fern Hill' by Dylan Thomas from *Dylan Thomas – Collected Poems,* eds Walford Davies and Ralph Maud (London: Phoenix, 2003)

'One Night I will Return to My Birthplace' by Majid Naficy from *MPT The Great Flight* No. 1 2016, translated by Elizabeth Gray

'Lower Market Street, 1973' by Lorna Thorpe from *A Ghost in My House* (Arc Publications, 2008)

'If I Were to Meet' by Grace Nichols from *Passport to Here and There* (Bloodaxe Books, 2020)

'Praise the Rain' by Joy Harjo from *Conflict Resolution for Holy Beings* (W. W. Norton & Co., 2015)

'rice & rain' by Robin Gow from *Poetry* magazine (November 2018, Poetry Foundation)

'The Breaking of The Drought' by Chris Magadza from *Father and other poems* (Poetry International Web, 2006)

'What friends are for' by Ann Sansom from *In Praise of Men and Other People* (Bloodaxe Books, 2003)

'Zephyr' by Catherine Smith from *Otherwhere* (Smith Doorstop, 2012)

'Diving into the Wreck' by Adrienne Rich from *Diving into the Wreck: Poems 1971-1972 by Adrienne Rich* (W. W. Norton & Co., 1973)

'Feast in Candlelight' by Fadhil Al Azzawi from *Miracle Maker: Selected Poems of Fadhil Al-Azzawi* (BOA Editions, Ltd., 2003)

'Glory Be to the Gang Gang Gang' by Momtaza Mehr. from *Poetry* magazine (April 2019, Poetry Foundation)

Chapter 14

'I am the song' by Charles Causley from *I am the song: Collected Poems 1951-2000* (Picador, 2000)

'I am Taliesin' translated by Sir Ifor Williams from *The School Bag* eds Seamus Heaney and Ted Hughes (Faber, 1997)

'Song Path' and 'Seven Days Walking and Seven Nights Camping in a Wood Scotland March 1985' by Hamish Fulton are from the print series 'Ten Toes towards the Rainbow 1985-92'

'Ovidian Flowers' by Ian Hamilton Finlay from *Ian Hamilton Finlay Selections*, ed. Alec Finlay (University of California Press, 2012)

Bibliography

Abani, Chris, *Kalakuta Republic* (Saqi Books, 2000)
Ackerman, Diane, *A Natural History of the Senses* (Vintage Books, 1992)
Al Azzawi, Fadhil, *Miracle Maker: Selected Poems of Fadhil Al-Azzawi* (BOA Editions, 2003)
Alvi, Moniza, *Split World: Poems 1990–2005* (Bloodaxe Books, 2008)
Alvi, Moniza, *At the Time of Partition* (Bloodaxe Books, 2013)
Agbabi, Patience, *Telling Tales* (Canongate, 2015)
Ara, Safuran, trans Debjani Chatterjee, *Songs in Exile/Probashir Pala: A bilingual collection* (Sheffield Libraries, 1999)
Bernard, Jay, *Surge* (Chatto & Windus, 2019)
Blake, William, *The Complete Poems* (Penguin Classics, 1977)
Brackenbury, Alison, *Dreams of Power* (Carcanet, 1981)
Brackenbury, Alison, *Then* (Carcanet, 2013)
Brownjohn, Sandy, *Does it Have to Rhyme?: Teaching Children to Rhyme* (Hodder Education, 1980)
Brooks, Gwendolyn, *Selected Poems* (Harper & Row, 1963)
Brooks, Gwendolyn, *The Bean Eaters* (Harper & Row, 1960)
Campbell, Roy (trans), *Poems of St John of the Cross* (Harvill, 1953)
Carson, Anne, *If Not, Winter: Fragments of Sappho* (Virago, 2003)
Caturbhani (written c. 300 BC): references made to *Glimpses of Sexual Life in Nanda-Maurya India*, an English translation of *Caturbhani* by Manomohan Ghosh (Manisha Granthalyaya Kolkota, 1975)
Causley, Charles, *I am the song: Collected Poems 1951–2000*, (Picador, 2000)
Clark, Thomas A, *To Scalasaig* (2000)
Darling, Julia, *Indelible, Miraculous: The collected poems of Julia Darling* (Arc Publications, 2015)
Day Lewis, Cecil, *Collected Poems of C Day Lewis* (Jonathan Cape with the Hogarth Press, 1954)
Dickinson, Emily, *The Complete Poems* (CreateSpace, 2015)
Duffy, Carol Ann, *Meeting Midnight* (Faber, 1999)
Duffy, Carol Ann, *Selling Manhattan* (Anvil Press Poetry, 1987)
Ellams, Inua, *Afterhours* (Nine Arches Press, 2017)
De Shong Meador, Betty, *Enheduanna, Princess, Priestess, Poet: The Sumerian Temple Hymns of Enheduanna* (University of Texas Press, 2009)
Evans, Martina, *Can Dentists Be Trusted?* (Anvil Press Poetry, 2004)
Evans, Martina, *All Alcoholics are Charmers* (Anvil Press Poetry, 1998)

Evans, Martina, *Burnfort, Las Vegas* (Anvil Press Poetry, 2014)
Fanthorpe, U A, *Selected Poems* (Peterloo Poets, 1986)
Feaver, Vicki, *The Book of Blood* (Jonathan Cape, 2006)
Feaver, Vicki, *The Handless Maiden* (Jonathan Cape, 1994)
Feaver, Vicki, *I Want! I Want!* (Jonathan Cape, 2019)
Feaver, Vicki, *Second Wind* (Saltire Society, 2015
Finlay, Ian Hamilton, *Evening Will Come They Will Sew the Blue Sail* (Graham Murray Edinburgh, 1998)
Finlay, Ian Hamilton, *Ian Hamilton Finlay Selections*, ed. Alec Finlay (University of California Press, 2012)
Forché, Carolyn, *The Country Between Us* (HarperCollins, 1981)
Ginsberg, Alan, *Howl and Other Poems* (City Lights, 1996)
Godden, Rumer, *A House with Four Rooms* (William Morrow & Co., 1989)
Godden, Rumer, *The Greengage Summer* (Macmillan & Co Ltd, 1958)
Graves, Robert, *The White Goddess* (Faber, 1999)
Hardi, Choman, *Considering the Women* (Bloodaxe Books, 2015)
Heaney, Seamus, *Haw Lantern* (Faber, 1987)
Hill, Selima, *Saying Hello at the Station* (Chatto & Windus, 1984)
Hill, Selima, *Gloria: Selected Poems* (Bloodaxe Books, 2008)
Hill, Selima, *Portrait of My Lover as a Horse* (Bloodaxe Books, 2002)
Hill, Selima, *Violet* (Bloodaxe Books, 1997)
Homer, *The Illiad* (written c. 8th century BC)
Hughes, Ted, *Collected Poems* (Faber, 2003)
Hughes, Ted, *Crow: From the Life and the Songs of the Crow* (Faber, 1970)
Jastrzębska, Maria, *Small Odysseys* (Waterloo Press, 2022)
Jin, Meiling, *Gifts from My Grandmother* (Sheba, 1985)
Johnson, Linton Kwesi, *Inglan is a Bitch* (Race Today Publications, 1981)
Johnson, Linton Kwesi, *Dread Beat An' Blood* (Bogle-L'Ouverture 1975)
Kamau Brathwaite, Edward, *The Arrivants: A New World Trilogy* (Oxford, 1981)
Khalvati, Mimi, *The Meanest Flower* (Carcanet, 2007)
Khalvati, Mimi, *Child: New and Selected Poems* (Carcanet, 2012)
Kay, Jackie, *Darling: New and Selected Poems* (Bloodaxe Books, 2007)
Kenny, Maurice, *They tell me I am lost, Harper's Anthology of Twentieth Century Native American Poetry* (1988)
Knight, Etheridge, *The Essential Etheridge Knight* (University of Pittsburgh Press, 1986)

Kramer, Lotte, *New and Collected Poems* (Rockingham Press, 2011)

Lewis, Gwyneth and Williams, Rowan (trans), *The Book of Taliesin* (Penguin, 2020)

Lochhead, Liz, *Dreaming Frankenstein and Collected Poems 1967–1984* (Polygon, 1984)

Longley, Michael, *Gorse Fires* (Jonathan Cape, 1991)

Lorde, Audre, *Sister Outsider* (The Crossing Press, 1984)

Mackay Brown, George, *The Collected Poems of George Mackay Brown* (John Murray, 2006)

MacNeice, Louise, *Collected Poems* (Faber, 1966)

Maguire, Sarah, *Almost the Equinox: Selected Poems* (Chatto & Windus, 2015)

Maguire, Sarah, *Spilt Milk* (Secker and Warburg, 1991)

Mitchell, Elma, *People Etcetera: New and Selected Poems* (Peterloo Poets, 1987)

Neruda, Pablo, trans. Ken Krabbenhoft, *Odes to Common Things* (Bulfinch; Illustrated edition, 1994)

Neruda, Pablo, trans. William O'Daly, *The Book of Questions* (Copper Canyon Press, 2001)

Nichols, Grace, *The Fat Black Woman's Poems* (Virago, 1986)

Nichols, Grace, *I Have Crossed an Ocean: Selected Poems* (Bloodaxe Books, 2010)

Nichols, Grace, *I Is a Long Memoried Woman* (Karnak House, 1983)

Olds, Sharon, *Satan Says* (University of Pittsburgh Press, 1980)

Olds, Sharon, *Stag's Leap* (Jonathan Cape, 2012)

Olds, Sharon, *The Matter of This World: New and Selected Poems* (Slow Dancer Press, 1987)

Padel, Ruth, *Darwin – A Life in Poems* (Random House, 2012)

Petit, Pascale, *What the Water Gave Me: Poems after Frieda Kahlo* (Seren, 2010)

Plath, Sylvia, *The Bell Jar* (Penguin, 1966)

Popa, Vasko, *Selected Poems* (Penguin, 1969)

Popa, Vasko, 'The Quartz Pebble', trans. Anne Pennington, *Complete Poems 1953–87* (Anvil, 2011)

Quraishi, Shazea, *The Courtesan's Reply* (Flipped Eye Publishing, 2012)

Rankin, Claudia, *Citizen* (Penguin, 2015)

Rees-Jones, Deryn, *Burying the Wren* (Seren, 2012)

Rouzeau, Valérie, trans. Susan Wicks, *Cold Spring in Winter (Pas Revoir)* (Arc Publications, 2010)

Sandburg, Carl, *The Complete Poems of Carl Sandburg* (Harcourt Brace, 1970)

Sansom, Peter, *Writing Poems* (Bloodaxe Poetry Handbooks, 1993)

Senior, Olive, *Gardening in the Tropics* (Insomniac Press, 2005)

Shakespeare, William, *Shakespeare's Measure for Measure* (Wordsworth Editions, 1995)

Smith, Catherine, *Otherwhere* (Smith|Doorstop, 2012)

Smith, Stevie, *The Collected Poems and Drawings of Stevie Smith* (Faber, 2015)

Shuttle, Penelope, *Sandgrain and Hourglass* (Bloodaxe Books, 2010)

Shuttle, Penelope, *Redgrove's Wife* (Bloodaxe Books, 2006)

Shuttle, Penelope, *Unsent: New and Selected Poems* (Bloodaxe Books, 2012)

Stainer, Pauline, *The Honeycomb* (Bloodaxe Books, 1989)

Stainer, Pauline, *Parable Island* (Bloodaxe Books, 1999)

Sutherland, Janet, *Home Farm* (Shearsman Books, 2019)

Szymborska, Wisława, trans. S. Baranczak & C. Cavanagh, *View with a grain of sand: selected poems* (Faber, 1995)

St Vincent Millay, Edna, *Collected Poems* (Harper Collins, 2011)

Taylor, Ross, *Captive Voices: New and Selected Poems 1960-2008* (Louisiana State Press, 2009)

Thomas, Edward, *Edward Thomas: Collected Poems* (Faber, 2004)

Thomas, Edward, *Last Poems* (Selwyn & Blount, 1918)

Thorpe, Lorna, *A Ghost in My House* (Arc Publications, 2008)

Thorpe, Lorna, *Sweet Torture of Breathing* (Arc Publications, 2011)

Twitchell, Chase, *The Snow Watcher* (Bloodaxe Books, 1999)

Williams, William Carlos, *Pictures from Breughel and other poems* (New Directions, 1967)

Wood, Lorna, *Ameliaranne Goes Digging* (George Harrap, 1948)

Xiaoni, Wang, trans. Eleanor Goodman, *Something Crosses My Mind* (Zephyr Press, 2014)

Xiaoni, Wang, trans. Gordon T. Osing and De-An Wu Swihart, *At the Edge of a Field, a Pair of Shoes* (Salt Hill, 1998)

Yosano, Akiko, *Tangled Hair: Selected Tanka from Midaregami* (Purdue University Studies, 1971)

Zhuangzi, *Chuang Tzŭ* (written 476-221 BC)

Anthologies

A Dangerous Knowing: Four Black Women Poets (Sheba Feminist Press, 1984)

Against Forgetting: 20th Century Poetry of Witness, edited by Carolyn Forché (W. W. Norton, 1993)

The Bible: Authorised King James Version (OUP Oxford; Illustrated edition, 2008)

The Bloodaxe Book of Modern Welsh Poetry : 20th-century Welsh-language poetry in translation (Bloodaxe Books, 2003)

Don't Ask Me What I Mean, edited by Clare Brown and Don Paterson (Picador, 2003)

Emergency Kit, edited by Jo Shapcott & Matthew Sweeney (Faber 1996)

Flora Poetica, edited by Sarah Maguire (Chatto & Windus, 2001)

Georgian Poetry, edited by James Reeves (Penguin, 1966)

Junior Voices The Second Book, edited by Geoffrey Summerfield (Penguin Books, 1970)

The Making of a Poem: A Norton Anthology of Poetic Forms, edited by Eavan Boland & Mark Strand (W. W. Norton, 2001)

The Mersey Sound, edited by Brian Patten, Roger McGough and Adrian Henri (Penguin Books, 1967)

Morning, Can I buy a slice of sky? edited by Grace Nichols (Blackie, 1991)

TEN New Poets Spread the Word (Bloodaxe Books, 2010)

Naming the Waves: Contemporary Lesbian Poetry by Christian McEwen (Virago, 1988)

News for Babylon: Book of West Indian British Poetry, edited by James Berry (Chatto 1984)

Pain into Poetry, Lotte Kramer, ARTEMISpoetry (Issue 2, May 2009), Second Light Publications

Penguin Modern Poets 8: Edwin Brock, Geoffrey Hill and Stevie Smith (Penguin Books, 1966)

Poetry of Witness: The Tradition in English, edited by Carolyn Forché & Duncan Wu (W. W. Norton, 2014)

Watchers and Seekers: Creative writing by Black Women in Britain, edited by Rhonda Cobham and Merle Collins (The Women's Press, 1987)

Acknowledgements

Every effort has been made to trace copyright holders and to obtain their permission for the use of copyrighted material. We would be pleased to rectify any omissions in subsequent editions should they be drawn to our attention.

Thank you to the following publishers, authors and literary estates for granting permission to reprint these poems:

'Thoughts after Ruskin' by Elma Mitchell is reprinted from *People Etcetera: New and Selected Poems* (1987) with kind permission from Hannah Elliot.

'Lapwings' by Alison Brackenbury is reprinted from *Then* (2013) with kind permission from Carcanet.

'Being Fifty' by Selima Hill is reprinted from *Violet* (1997) with kind permission from Bloodaxe Books.

'The Fat Black Woman Goes Shopping' by Grace Nichols is reprinted from *The Fat Black Woman's Poems* (1984) with kind permission from Little Brown.

'More fun than Nigella' by Lorna Thorpe is reprinted from *Sweet Torture of Breathing* (2011) with kind permission from Arc Publications.

'11 The Camp' by Moniza Alvi is reprinted from *At the Time of Partition* (2013) with kind permission from Bloodaxe Books.

'Zaatar' is reprinted from *Almost the Equinox* by Sarah Maguire published by Chatto & Windus. Copyright © Sarah Maguire 1991, 1997, 2001, 2007. Reproduced by permission of The Random House Group Ltd.

'The Doll's House' by Patience Agbabi is reprinted with kind permission from the author.

'Pepys and a Nightingale', copyright © Janet Sutherland, 2019. Taken from Janet Sutherland, Home Farm (Bristol: Shearsman Books, 2019).

'Hiss' by Jay Bernard is reprinted from *Surge* (2019) with kind permission from Chatto & Windus.

'The Fitting' by Edna St Vincent Millay (*Poetry Magazine*, 1938) is reprinted with kind permission from the Millay Foundation.

'The Fall' by Pauline Stainer is reprinted from *Parable Island* (1999) with kind permission from Bloodaxe Books.

'The Bean Eaters' by Gwendolyn Brooks is reprinted from *Selected Poems* (1963) with kind permission from Brooks Permissions.

'How To Behave With The Ill' by Julia Darling is reprinted from *Indelible, Miraculous: The Collected Poems of Julia Darling* (2015) with kind permission from Arc Publications.

'Gazebo' by Martina Evans is reprinted from *Burnfort, Las Vegas* (2014) with kind permission from Carcanet.

'Lunch', copyright © Lotte Kramer, 2015. Taken from Lotte Kramer, *More New & Selected Poems* (Rockingham Press, 2015).

'On the 70th Anniversary of the Warsaw Uprising' by Maria Jastrzębska is reprinted from *Small Odysseys* (2022) with kind permission from Waterloo Press.

'A Bengali Woman in Britain' by Safuran Ara (trans. Debjani Chatterjee) is reprinted from *Songs in Exile/Probashir Pala: A bilingual collection* (1999) with kind permission from Debjani Chatterjee.

Further Resources for Writers

Places to Read and Listen to Poems Online

Academy of American Poets: including Poem-A-Day daily newsletter
African Poems.net
A Poem a Week (podcast)
Badlisha Poetry (developing online archive of contemporary African poets)
British Library: The Power of Caribbean Poetry (sound recordings)
First World War Poetry digital archive
Library of Congress (US): Archive of Recorded Poetry and Literature
Library of Congress (US): Living Nations, Living Words (recordings of contemporary Native Nations poets)
Oxford Brookes Poetry Centre: weekly poem
The Poetry Archive: Transport for London (poems of the day)
The Poetry Foundation
Poetry International (searchable by country and language)
The Poetry Review website
Scottish Poetry Library

Advice and Writer Development

The Manchester Poetry Library
National Poetry Library: Write & Publish
The Scottish Poetry Library
Writers & Artists: Resources
The Arvon Foundation
Hive South Yorkshire
Moniack Mhor
National Association of Writers in Education (NAWE)
New Writing North
New Writing South
The Poetry Business
Poetry London: Courses
The Poetry School
Poetry Society Stanzas (available to anyone who is already a member of the Poetry Society)
Spread the Word
Tŷ Newydd, Literature Wales
The Writing Squad (for young people in the North of England)
Writing West Midlands

Funding

Arts Council England

Arts Council of Ireland
Arts Council of Wales
Creative Scotland
The Northern Writers' Awards
The Royal Literary Fund
The Society of Authors

Submissions, News and Listings

National Poetry Library (including poetry magazine listings)
NAWE Writers' Compass
Poetry London Listings
The Poetry Kit
Poetry School: Places to Submit Your Poetry
Robin Houghton Poetry (email newsletter)